Using Vintage Hymns in Worship

*Hidden Treasures Rediscovered
for Today's Church*

— GILLIAN R. WARSON —

Sacristy Press
PO Box 612, Durham, DH1 9HT

www.sacristy.co.uk

First published in 2021 by Sacristy Press, Durham

Sacristy Limited, registered in England & Wales, number 7565667

British Library Cataloguing-in-Publication Data
A catalogue record for the book is available
from the British Library

ISBN 978-1-78959-164-4

Contents

Introduction

Recently, when I was selecting hymns for a worship resource, the editors told me in no uncertain terms that I could not choose "All things bright and beautiful". "That's not relevant for singers in the twenty-first century!" But what could be so wrong with this popular hymn that it should be rejected out of hand? In any case, what did they mean by "relevant"? This led me to wonder what could be the general criteria for deciding whether this or that hymn is "relevant" or not. We all know that "All things bright and beautiful" (Cecil Frances Alexander, née Humphreys, 1818–95) has been sung on countless occasions in all manner of settings including churches, schools, crematoria, nursing homes and hospitals. It is published in numerous hymnbooks, and there are countless people who can sing it from memory. Strange, then, that it should be considered unsuitable for singing today! This set me thinking, and this book is the result of those thoughts.

People sing hymns for many reasons. For Christian believers, hymns offer an opportunity to bear witness to their faith and lift their voices in praise with their fellow-worshippers. But whether we are believers or non-believers, we can all enjoy singing a favourite hymn as this intimate union of text and music lifts our spirits. Furthermore, singing hymns joins us with a living tradition that stretches back across the centuries and also connects us with our past selves as we sing these self-same hymns. Beyond this powerful sense of sharing—with others, with a historical past and with our past selves—there is a further dimension to our experience to be explored. As society changes, so do our social attitudes with the result that we may come to view any hymn text from an entirely new perspective. In fact, there are at least two points of view to be taken into account when we consider the meaning or worth of a hymn. The first is the point of view of the hymn writers along with their intended singers at the specific point in history when the hymn was written. The second point of view is that of later singers who confront each hymn from the perspective of their own age, with all the beliefs and attitudes of society at that time. Therefore, later singers may interpret the original text in a way quite different from that of the original writer. Indeed, as we shall see, the meaning understood by later singers may be quite at odds with the hymn writer's original intention! It is not only hymns, of course, that are reinterpreted and re-evaluated in this way: all art and literature sits on the shifting sands of cultural change. In 2020, the discussion surrounding colonial relics is of particular interest with the consideration of darker aspects of history. Nevertheless, however much our sensibilities may have changed, we must recognize that the ideas that speak to us through a hymn, expressed in these specific words wedded to this particular music, can display a special power not only to move our emotions, but even to impel us to act on what we feel. For this reason, I shall be arguing that hymns, even those dulled by familiarity, far from being trite and complacent, have the power not only to alert us to grave dangers facing the world today, but even to move us to decisive action.

It is tempting to disregard older hymns, thinking of them as past their sell-by date, yet, for many of the faithful, these traditional texts have come to form the bedrock of worship and liturgy. Others, even those who do not go to church, may be reminded of the enjoyable circumstances when and where they first sang the hymns. Therefore, I shall be blowing the dust off unfashionable texts and arguing that they can now be regarded as what I shall call "vintage". Can anything match the excitement of stumbling on a forgotten, but previously well-loved item, waiting to be rediscovered? Our hymns are just the same—not everything languishing at the back of the cupboard is a lost treasure, and can be quietly forgotten. Indeed, out of the 6000 hymns by Charles Wesley, how many are sung today? I will be exploring the different places in which we encounter hymns in our everyday lives, including popular music, novels, films and television. Does finding hymns in so many different places reduce their appeal by overfamiliarity?

This is a question we shall be addressing later. In the course of this discussion, we will also delve into the rich resource that we recognize as a hymnbook. There are difficulties, though, in continuing to sing hymns that for many reasons no longer speak to us because of changes in social attitudes. We shall ask how hymns that raise thorny issues about race, patriarchy, empire, warfare or gender should be dealt with. How, for instance, can we continue to cherish hymns that give voice to attitudes we no longer wish to share? Do we discard them and risk impoverishing this rich legacy? We will consider how hymn singing can continue as a flourishing tradition with old and new coexisting comfortably alongside each other. In order for this to happen, we have to acknowledge that, putting our personal preferences to one side, our vintage texts need to be lovingly preserved so that they can be enjoyed for countless generations to come.

CHAPTER 1

The tradition of hymn singing

Why sing hymns?

To find an answer to this question, first we need to establish what we understand by a "hymn". Then we are in a position to ask why we sing hymns at all.

As with most words, too strict a definition will be certain to exclude what many people would recognize as a hymn—or include examples that others would reject out of hand! Thomas Aquinas (c.1225–74) defines the Christian hymn as being the "praise of God with song; a song is the exultation of the mind dwelling on eternal things, bursting forth in the voice".[1] This definition could be a useful point of departure, but would exclude many examples of sung verses that have no explicit reference to God yet are regarded by many singers as "hymns" in a wider sense. As a first step towards a flexible working definition of a "hymn" for the purposes of this discussion, I shall define a hymn as a set of verses set to music intended—initially, at least—to be sung by a congregation in celebration of truths enshrined in the Christian faith. Here, I am excluding sacred choral works meant for performance by a choir, such as the large-scale oratorios and masses. By "the truths enshrined in the Christian faith", I mean to include both traditional hymns where there is explicit reference to God, as well as people and places mentioned in the Bible, and sung verses that express moral sentiments, such as love of neighbour, promoting peace and avoiding violence and so on. These ideas are wholly in tune with Christian belief but feature no explicit reference to "holy" characters and places. For example, "One more step along the world I go" (Sydney Carter, 1905–2004) is included in many hymnbooks and widely acknowledged as a hymn—yet has none of the vocabulary we recognize as religious. I include the proviso "initially, at least" in acknowledgement of the fact that, though most hymns are written in the first instance to be sung by a church congregation, they can move beyond the church and be sung by people who play no part in formal church worship. Even if we cannot agree on the exact definition of a hymn, we all know one when we hear one! For some people of faith, a hymn is the expression of a spiritual message and can be part of their personal journey. For others, though, a hymn is something quite different, a shared experience either in large or small groups perhaps marking a rite of passage. This is why we sing hymns. Singing together—whether hymns or any other songs—is a unique experience and can help express a collective response to all manner of situations. From protest songs speaking out against injustice and hatred to the chanting of a football crowd, the power of collective singing can stir up emotions. The blend of text and tune means that when we sing a hymn there is an opportunity not only to think about what the words mean but also to feel the force of these words as conveyed by the music. This goes some way to explain the mysterious power that hymns can exert—a power that extends far beyond the church and even beyond the text and the tune—a power that is able to influence, for good or evil, our conduct and attitudes.

Old-fashioned or vintage?

There are certain hymns which we know and love, and many of these have been in circulation for hundreds of years. It would be a very long book indeed if every well-loved hymn was to be discussed. Some singers favour traditional hymns which have been enjoyed for centuries, and others remember their school days, joining in with classmates for a rousing sing. Furthermore, there are considerations regarding denominational and cultural preferences. In spite of their apparent popularity, some of these hymns, even so, are starting to fall from favour and are branded as "out-of-date" and "old-fashioned". We know, however, that "old" and "old-fashioned" are not the same thing. The *Oxford English Dictionary* tells us that "old-fashioned" means "formed or conducted according to the fashion of former times" and is, in this case, "out of use" and "obsolete". It is this idea that

I want to challenge as we explore the reasons why we might want to keep or reject a given hymn. It would be quite in order to discard something as "obsolete" and start with something new. However, if, rather than "old-fashioned", we consider using the word "vintage", we then have something that is certainly old but worth preserving and even treasuring. It is by keeping the word "vintage" in mind that I want to assess whether or not some of our best-known hymns are worthy of preserving. Our attitude to an old thing is powerfully influenced by considering whether it can still perform its original function. We might, for example, throw out an "old-fashioned" washing machine because a new model performs the function of washing clothes more efficiently. On the other hand, we may be happy to keep an old chair because it continues to fulfil its original purpose in that it is comfortable to sit on and attractive. Thus, it is not the "oldness" of a hymn that is the crucial feature when deciding to retain or reject it, but whether it continues to fulfil its original purpose. Perhaps, rather than asking whether or not a hymn is "old-fashioned", we should ask if it touches our hearts and fires our imaginations—then it is surely worthy of retaining its place as a vintage hymn.

Our original question concerned the criteria for keeping or rejecting a hymn on the grounds of relevance, and it is on this particular point that I shall concentrate. A hymn may display several different kinds of features that lead us to hold on to it. Is it couched in especially beautiful language? Is it significant because of the author's reputation? Does it have important historical or cultural associations? Is it a striking expression of a deep and abiding truth for Christians? It is our response to questions such as these that will influence us when we decide to preserve a particular hymn.

Just for church?

One of the interesting things about hymns is how they have a life of their own outside church and conventionally religious settings. It could be said that singing hymns— or at least knowing some hymns—is important for many people irrespective of their attitudes to religion and regardless of the spiritual content of the texts. This reveals that hymns have a cultural significance beyond the religious. Most Christian denominations in England are steeped in their own traditions that can be seen in the variety of liturgical rituals, dress codes and in the buildings themselves. These things are unfamiliar to those who do not attend church, and even churchgoers from one denomination may look askance at the practices of another. This means that the rich tradition of hymn singing in England is distinct from other church rituals. Although generally associated with Christianity by virtue of their essential Christian imagery and content, hymns take on a parallel importance by being embedded in a wider cultural context. The very fact that hymns are sung on numerous secular occasions shows that, far from being "obsolete" and "old-fashioned", they are loved and treasured—thus ensuring their status as "vintage".

In our quest to search out "relevant" hymns, it would be easy to include all hymns that are popular. We might be surprised when someone does not know— or like—a hymn of which we are particularly fond. If something is popular, it means that it is popular among a certain group: what is popular with one group may be anathema to another. Audiences vary and may include, for example, at one extreme those who never miss a church service and at the other people who have never been inside a church. One telling measure of a hymn's popularity, however, is the extent to which it has burst out of its conventional church setting and is found in altogether unlikely places. Michael Saward (1932–2015), writer of "Christ Triumphant", told me in a conversation in 2011 that he really knew that he had arrived when his hymn could be heard in the background in Pauline Fowler's kitchen in an episode of *EastEnders*. More obvious instances of hymns in popular culture can be found in pop music, and some of the significant hymn "hits" of the 1970s remain known and loved to us today. These include Elvis Presley's version of "How Great Thou Art" (Stuart K. Hine, 1899–1989) and Cat Stevens' "Morning has broken" (Eleanor Farjeon, 1881–1965). Beyond the world of popular music, hymns often pop up in the most unexpected places, and many people have tales to tell about how they encountered a hymn where they least expected it. One telling measure of a hymn's popularity is how often it is mentioned in literature that is not chiefly concerned with church matters. Novels, for example, give us many clues about the social and cultural milieu in which they were first written and often include references to hymns. In early novels, these are largely restricted to situations and characters associated with religious observance. This is not surprising because the vast majority of readers of these novels would have been churchgoers, and it is not unusual for whole verses of a hymn to be reproduced faithfully along with details about how and where they were sung. For example, *The Expedition of Humphry Clinker*, by Tobias Smollett, tells us about the world of the Nonconformist preacher as he "lines out" the Psalms. George Eliot, too, often sprinkles telling references to hymns in her novels as a means of distinguishing between Anglicans and Methodists. In *Adam Bede*, we first meet the Anglican Adam early in the novel as he sings Bishop Ken's (1637–1711) "Morning Hymn" in his workshop. The Methodist preacher Dinah Morris, on the other hand, restricts her hymn singing to leading worship and teaching. Charlotte Brontë, too, had an eye for detail in the presentation of hymns, especially in her novel *Shirley*, which makes her a reliable source of information. For readers today who may well not attend church, however, the mention of hymns continues to provide a telling indication that they were really important to these novelists and their readers.

These earlier novels show hymns in a religious setting. However, novelists gradually grew so confident that their readers would be familiar with hymns that they were able to weave a hymn text into their story to add colour and interest in order to illustrate situations on which religion had little bearing. This clearly shows that the reading public was no longer assumed to be a church-attending public, and that hymns themselves had come to mean many things to many people. The novels of Howard Spring (1889–1968) are a fine example of this. His two early successes, *O Absalom* and *Fame is the Spur,* are peppered with quotations from hymns. Here hymns are used not only to express religious fervour, but also to reflect political struggle, social change and personal dilemmas.

Throughout the twentieth century, novelists continued to use hymns to illustrate aspects of both plot and everyday life. There is a clear assumption that the reader would be familiar with the words of hymns, but their secular context makes it increasingly obvious that their spiritual message is not the principal point. Barbara Pym (1913–80) uses the Anglican Church as a backdrop for her novels and weaves words from hymns into the text in a gentle, evocative way that has little to do with the hymn writers' original vision of salvation. In her case, everyday objects call to mind a line from a hymn, thus showing how novelists, whilst recognizing that their readers might well be familiar with hymns, acknowledged they would not necessarily mean to these same readers what they once meant to churchgoers in the past. Hymns find their way into books from classics to detective novels with examples far too numerous to mention. This, though, is worthy of note for reasons which extend beyond the oddly satisfying feeling of "I know that!" Encountering them in a non-religious situation can even lead us to interpret their meaning in a different way.

Hymns, then, can be found in all sorts of places when we are least looking for them. Where, then, have we learned these hymns that are so familiar? Although attendance at church has been falling steadily in recent decades, there is strong evidence that hymns remain important to many people. *Songs of Praise*, for example, has been broadcast on the BBC since 1961 and is the longest-running series of such a programme anywhere in the world. It has been viewed by many millions of people, all tuning in to enjoy their favourite hymns. Where did people learn these hymns if not from church? They learned them at school. Although not all schools have a time for corporate Christian worship, it is not unusual for local ministers of various denominations to visit schools to lead an assembly. Many, but not all, schools in England actively celebrate Christmas and Easter with singing and drama, and harvest festivals can play a major part in the autumn term each academic year. It is here that we find our favourite hymns forming a vast repository of memory as a result of repetition in our formative years. From the school hall, these hymns then go on to form a core repertoire for rites of passage including weddings, baptisms and funerals. Some hymns become personal favourites "handed down" from one generation to another for family occasions. However, one less welcome outcome of having a favourite hymn is that it may be chosen at random for a given occasion whether or not it is deemed entirely suitable by the cognoscenti! It is, perhaps, for this reason that ministers are given to groaning at yet another request for "All things bright and beautiful".

Familiarity = contempt?

Does the very familiarity of a hymn make it less relevant for contemporary hymn singers? In fact, it could be that some singers are wary of, even embarrassed by admitting that they enjoy a particular hymn. I would argue that a vital aspect of our tradition of hymn singing lies in this very familiarity. For some, "familiarity breeds contempt"—an attitude that sometimes manifests itself in the case of familiar hymns. In some circumstances, the more we know something, the more we may treat it with disdain, finding fault with it and even coming to dislike it. However, there can be no question that familiar hymns—though sometimes the object of scorn—resonate deep within our psyche and that repeated singing enables them to conjure up a host of feelings and associations. These may include memories of singing in school, perhaps on special occasions, and at those times we can sing with the voice of our past selves. As we join our voices to those of others, we can feel the deep-seated power of the hymn within us. This leads, however, to a further question. Following our working definition of a hymn as a set of verses set to music sung in celebration of moral truths espoused by Christians, are we licensed to assume that, when a hymn is sung by a group of singers, all those singers subscribe to the broadly Christian "message" intended by the hymn's author? In other words, when hymn singers join together for a jolly good sing, is it certain that the words of the hymn mean the same to each of them?

Once more as we consider the relevance of our vintage hymns, we need to think about what happens to the meaning of the words when they are sung and resung in different contexts. What might happen is that different singers may, for good or evil, interpret the words that they are singing in quite different—perhaps even opposing—ways. Who can forget a drugged and drunk but staunchly illiberal Alice in the 2020 television series *Mrs America* (first premiered FX on Hulu) happily singing along to "This land is my land" on the grounds that it was "patriotic" in the company of a group of lesbians, with whom she shared no solidarity whatsoever. Both groups claimed the same text as their own but for different reasons. However, very often the meaning of the words escapes the groups of singers in the thrill of the occasion. An obvious example of this is communal singing as heard at sporting events where, just because everyone is singing the same words, it does not follow that each singer either understands the meaning of the text in the same way or shares the same feelings when singing. The annual rendition of "Abide with me" (H. F. Lyte, 1793–1847) at the FA Cup Final is a case in point. It was sung for the first time in the stadium in 1927 and since then has added to the excitement of the event. Whilst there is no doubt that, in accordance with our definition of a hymn, "Abide with me" fits the bill, on these occasions the mass singing is not an example of religious fervour, but evidence of a swell of a genuine feeling of togetherness and belonging. Here at the football match—assuming you can afford the ticket—there is no separation of wealth, social class or education.

However, wrapped inside the musical activity of hymn singing are, of course, words—words that people may sing without thinking. This brings us to the darker side of mass hymn singing. Singing together is, of course, a lovely thing to do and can give us that warm fuzzy feeling. Equally though, along with any group activity, hymn singing can be divisive. History has shown us that large groups of people singing—even holy words—can be sinister, even frightening. It could also be that whilst one group enjoys a rousing sing, unwitting offence is being caused to another. For example, in the midst of the "Black Lives Matter" discussions of 2020, the spiritual "Swing Low, Sweet Chariot" made its way into the headlines. Well-known as England's unofficial rugby anthem, fans sing it with gusto although, of course, it has connections with slavery and what many believe to be the continuing oppression of people of colour. It is difficult to imagine a rugby match without this rousing anthem ringing out from around the pitch, yet there is unease in some quarters. Although the song's future in this context has been questioned, no decisive response has yet been agreed beyond a vague suggestion that its true history should be made more widely known. It may be argued that this lack of action betrays moral ambivalence, but perhaps this public debate will lead to more careful thought about what we sing in the future.

Hymn singing is one of our important traditional activities. Tradition, however, can be viewed in many different ways. Indeed, the very idea of a tradition can excite both warm approval or deep suspicion: is tradition a comforting link with the past such as handing recipes down through a family or dancing round the maypole, or is it a backward-looking determination to maintain the status quo? We all know that traditional activities and customs are not always good and can sometimes even involve glorifying events of which we are now ashamed. Just because something is familiar, it does not make it good. The crucial question here, though, is whether we want to remove all traces of our history—even those which are unpalatable to us. The argument in favour of maintaining tradition speaks against the flattening of difference and warns of the inevitable metropolitan uniformity that would result. We have already said that one of the important reasons for singing hymns is that it brings us together—whether on the sports field, in a secular environment or even, dare I say it, in church. Whilst there is undoubtedly evidence in some of our vintage hymns of outdated language and prejudice, there are, as we shall see, many reasons why we may continue to sing many of these older hymns with a clear conscience. A specific example of this is "The day thou gavest, Lord, is ended", which was written in 1870 by John Ellerton (1826–93). It is published in countless hymnbooks starting with *Hymns Ancient & Modern* (1875). Some may feel its language is outdated, based as it is on the rhetoric of the Empire over which "the sun never sets". However, it goes on to claim that ultimately the kingdom of God will endure even after "earth's proud empires pass away". Clearly a product of its time, written at the height of Victorian imperialism, the idea of empire and the kingdom of God sit comfortably together. This shows that it is not always easy to decide if a text has had its day or not. Since it soared to popularity when it was heard at Queen Victoria's Diamond Jubilee, it has been sung on countless significant occasions. It was used at the ceremony when Hong Kong was handed back to China in 1997, and even selected as the international hymn for the World Day of Prayer in 2016, which demonstrates its power as an inclusive rather than exclusive text. Now chosen for countless family, civic and state occasions as well as often used in church services, it seems very unlikely that this hymn will be joining others on the scrap heap any time soon.

What can we learn from the past?

Singing vintage hymns can play an important part in defining our cultural identity. This is one reason why, instead of discarding our older hymns as "old-fashioned", we should preserve them for future generations. However, older hymns have a role to play far beyond this. We can learn something valuable from the historical context in which older hymns have been written. Some of our finest hymn writers were also conscientious preachers and Sunday school teachers whose pedagogical skills have made their texts fine teaching tools. We know, for example, that John Newton (1725–1807) preached to huge congregations where many of his hymns were used to explain the text of the day. It is also clear that the very same dilemmas we face today were also confronted by the writers of older hymns. This means that their hymns may have a startling contemporary relevance even in our present age, when we cannot escape dire warnings of food poverty, climate change and diminishing biodiversity. In our eagerness to confront these matters, as well as to speak up for those who have no voice of their own and make amends for our past wrongs, one response could be to write new hymns. Certainly, there are many fine, newly minted texts which draw attention to our problems. However, there are also plenty of vintage hymns that can make sure we retain a vivid awareness of the questions of our age and perhaps spur us to respond in our day-to-day lives. An example of an inspiring hymn on the subject of Christian action is "Soldiers of Christ arise" by Charles Wesley (1707–88). In this text, every line is a challenge set alongside an assurance of the ever-present help and strength from God:

> Stand then in His great might,
> with all His strength endued;
> And take, to arm you for the fight,
> the panoply of God;
> that, having all things done,
> and all your conflicts passed
> Ye may o'ercome through Christ alone
> and stand entire at last.

Furthermore, we can continue to treasure our vintage hymns through singing and resinging them, to make sure they are still available for generations to come.

Why hymnbooks?

It is not unusual for people to be able to sing hymns by heart—even if they don't know they know them! When the earliest hymns were written, of course, a lack of universal literacy prevented congregations from reading the texts. This means that hymn singing, along with other folk traditions, developed from an oral tradition. However, this has not been the case for several hundred years. If we are not relying on a purely oral tradition, there needs to be a convenient way of preserving and passing down our hymns: this is the hymnbook. The earliest hymnbooks had a rocky time because of political and liturgical opposition to texts which were not direct paraphrases of scripture. Following the versification of the Psalms, official disapproval was gradually relaxed and over time several weighty volumes of hymns became accepted. Of the many hymnbooks available to singers across the centuries, perhaps some were more influential than others. Wesley's book *A Collection of Hymns, for the People called Methodists* (1779) and *Hymns Ancient & Modern* (1861) enjoy particular status, but this, of course, is a matter of personal opinion and taste! The generally accepted definition of a "hymnbook" is a published collection of hymn texts (with or without tunes) usually by various authors covering a wide range of subjects. Hymns have appeared in non-religious collections—further evidence that hymn singing can be enjoyed as an activity in its own right—but a hymnbook is far more than a mere book of songs. Not only does it record hymns, but also plays a vital role in the traditions of the Church. Since hymnbooks have always played a central part in worship, it is worth pausing to consider what a hymnbook itself might actually represent to the congregation for which it was intended. Hymnbooks (or hymnals) fulfil many purposes. For many denominations, particularly Nonconformists, the hymnbook represents a vital liturgical resource second only in importance to the Bible. All worshipping communities would recognize the place of the hymnbook as a teaching tool able to communicate biblical and theological truths with clarity and economy. The presence of a hymnbook can be a source of comfort in difficult times. It is true that many churches have moved away from using hymnbooks in favour of screens, but for some the printed words remain an essential part of the singing experience.

What can we learn from the fact that a hymn has been published in a hymnbook? If the hymn has not been published before, it indicates that the author and publisher think that it will appeal to its intended audience of singers in so far as it will serve a useful role in their worship. However, if a hymn has already appeared in print and is to be published yet again in a new hymnbook, this is a clear indication of its enduring popularity over time. And so, the appearance—or disappearance—of a hymn from hymnbooks provides a useful measure of how a hymn text has been received by different generations of singers. This test can also be used to reveal how hymns may not be considered popular and relevant because they fall by the wayside as new hymnbooks are compiled. Hymnbooks themselves are durable and the hymns they contain can be sung by the purchasing community without the need to make any further payments. The huge financial outlay of furnishing a whole group with individual books is not undertaken lightly, and it is usual to find churches and schools that have not replaced their regular volume for many years. Whilst it is very comforting to sit in the pews leafing through an aged hymnbook remembering all the previous singers who have used it, some obvious difficulties arise if we continue to use old books. The chief drawback is the inevitably conservative nature of any collection and the fact that some of the hymn texts may, with the passing of time, start to express ideas, opinions and attitudes to which the current singers are no longer willing to subscribe. We shall be looking at this subject later, but it is worth stating that once a text appears in a printed hymnbook in whatever form the publisher thinks fit, it is there fixed for future generations to sing. Although using a dated hymnbook can be frustrating for those wishing to sing newer material, continuing to use an older volume means that it is less likely that the hymns we know and love will be lost. By continuing to sing from the printed book, especially an old one, we are connected with the singing community of the past.

Many singers can remember the hymnbook they used at school or church. This forms a key part in their collective memory of shared worship and aids the recollection of the hymns themselves even after the physical hymnbook is no longer in use. In fact, there are whole forums on the internet where singers share memories of their cherished hymns, remembering assemblies gathered around the piano as the music teacher thumps out a rousing accompaniment. This could all too easily be dismissed as simply learning by rote, but we have already established that hymns are texts full of meaning, and it is entirely possible that singers are, even subconsciously, taking this meaning into their daily lives. Of course, there are many different "flavours" of hymnbook, and this stems, in part, from denominational diversity. In spite of this, most singers are happy to sing familiar words whatever their source.

So, hymnbooks are vital to our hymn-singing tradition and to gauge their importance we can look beyond church and school into our wider culture. Once more novels can show us how hymnbooks became established in the mid-nineteenth century only to be ousted in the mid-twentieth century. For example, although it was not published until 1903, Samuel Butler (1835–1902) began writing *The Way of All Flesh* in 1873. In one short paragraph, Butler cleverly shows how Anglican hymn singing became dominated by one particular hymnbook. We read that the group of rustic musicians has been replaced by

> a harmonium played by a sweet-looking girl
> with a choir of school children around her, and
> they chanted the canticles to the most correct
> of chants, and they sang *Hymns Ancient &*
> *Modern.*[2]

This places Hymns Ancient & Modern firmly in its
historical context, but furthermore we are reminded that
novelists were confident that readers would be familiar
with hymns and the sources—i.e. hymnbooks—from
which they were drawn. A glimpse of an everyday object
can send a character back to their school hymnbook,
taking the reader with them. In *A Few Green Leaves* by
Barbara Pym, anthropologist Emma Howick notices a
brooch on the hat of the vicar's "char" which calls to
mind the hymn "Fierce was the wild billow, dark was
the night" (John Mason Neale, 1818–66), which she
remembers from the hymnbook she used at school, *The*
English Hymnal. This shows that hymns were appearing
in novels divorced from a purely church context in the
second half of the twentieth century. Nevertheless, in
a later book, *An Unsuitable Attachment*, Barbara Pym
reminds us of the more serious aspects of hymn singing.
We meet Ianthe Broome, a regular churchgoer, who is
most disapproving when a library colleague quotes from
a hymn with secular levity.

Novelists show that hymnbooks and their contents
find their place in the wider world. Gradually, in the
course of the past few decades, hymnbooks have been,

in some measure, replaced first by scraps of paper left in the pew, then by overhead projectors and finally by digital projectors. These innovations have been met with delight on one side and disgust on the other. So significant is this change that we can even read about it in late twentieth-century novels. In *A Price for Everything*, we meet the vestiges of a choir which consists of only one singer and a vicar who has a habit of altering the hymns at the last minute. One particular Sunday, instead of the traditional favourite, "Lead us, Heavenly Father, lead us" (James Edmeston, 1791–1867), the congregation "crossly" sang "a hymn so new, that it did not appear in the hymnbook and was printed on slips of paper in the pews".[3]

The dissatisfaction engendered by the "slips of paper" leads us to deduce that it is not only the hymns themselves but also hymnbooks that play a vital part in our hymn-singing tradition. One reason for this could be that the more "modern" we become, the more we want to hold on to everything associated with our cultural heritage. Hymnbooks belong to all who know and love their contents, regardless of whether or not they continue to use the volumes regularly. If we dispense with hymnbooks, there is a danger that some of our collective store of hymns will disappear with them.

CHAPTER 2

Keeping the tradition of hymn singing vibrant

To keep or not to keep?

So, the dusty hymnbooks at the back of the cupboard live on to fight another day! Is this discussion, though, simply a displacement activity so we don't have to do any tidying up? Absolutely not! Now we can start deciding which of our vintage hymns are relevant for singing today. In our day-to-day lives, we are urged to keep up to date, yet the darling of yesterday so often becomes the demon of today—and the pendulum swings back and forth. In the summer of 2020, the recommended use of disposable coffee cups provides a telling example of fluctuating attitudes. Prior to 2020, there was mounting pressure to shun these in favour of reusable cups, but then, with the threat of COVID-19 infection, single-use cups once more became the order of the day. The world of fashion offers a further example. Fashion-conscious dressers feel compelled to keep updating their wardrobe, and yet there is a countervailing wisdom that urges us to hold on to last year's vogue and wait for the style to re-enter the catwalks. How I am kicking myself for throwing out those flowery Doc Martens! Here is an example of vintage versus "old-fashioned". It is all too easy to think that something is no use because it is no longer in fashion. It is no different when we consider our hymns. One thing we can be sure of, though, is that the remorseless search for the new is literally costing the earth and to re-love and re-use makes good sense.

Is it, then, purely a matter of fashion that leads us to decide on the relevance of a hymn? Let's start by looking at the reasons why we may either keep or discard a hymn. One reason that a hymn may be discarded is because it is associated with an uninspiring tune. The marriage of texts to tunes is outside the scope of this book, but it is worth noting that the success and longevity of "Jerusalem" (William Blake, 1752–1827), which we will look at later, comes without doubt because it is linked to the stirring tune of the same name by C. H. H. Parry (1848–1918). We have also suggested that a hymn may be discarded simply because it can no longer be found in an available hymnbook. However, there are perhaps two more significant reasons why a hymn is deemed irrelevant and therefore to be discarded. The first is that the idea or sentiment in a hymn is, to singers today, unsatisfactory. As we shall see, we are now less comfortable singing hymns that describe the beauties of foreign climes such as "From Greenland's icy mountains" (Reginald Heber, 1783–1826) or "Hills of the north, rejoice" (Charles Edward Oakley, 1832–65) because, alongside the sumptuous descriptions, we confront the language of empire with the "home" of the fifth verse of the latter clearly referring to England! The further reason why a hymn might be deemed not relevant is that, whilst the idea or sentiment is acceptable to singers today, it may be couched in language in some sense unsatisfactory—for example, it may have obscure vocabulary, over-complex syntax, strained imagery or forced inversions.

Before moving on to discuss how we can continue to enjoy our vintage hymns, let's think about who might be making the decisions about the relevance, or not, of our vintage hymns. Is it the ordinary singer in the pew and the wider community who find a hymn no longer speaks to them? Perhaps church authorities feel that a specific hymn has a message from which they wish to distance themselves? Members of a church may feel that the text sends a message no longer acceptable to them. On the other hand, it could be, as we have seen, that individual ministers and worship leaders are simply tired of a hymn and can't be bothered with it anymore. Finally, it could be the choice of anxious hymnbook committees and publishers who no longer wish to associate themselves with what they consider to be a dated text.

It goes without saying, of course, that everything was new once. Even the hymns that seem to have been around for ever were ground-breaking in their day. For example, imagine a hymnbook which did not contain "Amazing Grace". Yet John Newton introduced this brand-new text on 1 January 1773 to assist his congregation in their understanding of the reading for the day. Now the hymn, perhaps one of the finest vintage hymns, has burst out of the pew into the realm of popular culture with Beyoncé performing it both as a soloist and with the group Destiny's Child. Mica Paris, indeed, has used this hymn, written by a former slave-trader, as an example of gospel music which moves both singers and audience alike to recognize racial injustice past and present.

How old does something have to be before it becomes vintage? We hear the expression, "the 70s, the decade taste forgot"—or was that the 80s, or even the 90s? By this token, it seems no time at all since "Shine, Jesus, shine (Lord, the light of your love is shining)" by Graham Kendrick (b. 1950) was new and exciting. Yet it has been published in hymnbooks since the early 1990s, nearly thirty years ago! One of these hymnbooks has the title *Hymns we have always loved*. As we ponder this title, we must surely ask ourselves how long ago is "always"? Some might say "Shine, Jesus, shine" has joined the ranks of tired texts now well past their sell-by date. Even so it is known and loved by many and is frequently chosen for weddings and baptisms. This shows that there are two radically different ways in which we can understand "always". First, we have a hymn that, in our personal experience, we have known for a long time—such as "Shine, Jesus, shine". Second, we have the vast store of hymns, including those such as "Amazing Grace", which have been sung across the centuries. The hymns of our schooldays become hymns which some people have "always" known even if they were written relatively recently. For others, hymns they have "always" known are those written well before their birth.

Why keep singing vintage hymns?

In our quest to seek out relevant hymns, let's start to explore some of the reasons for continuing to sing vintage hymns and assess how they can find new resonance in the twenty-first century. There are several ways we can respond in our hymns to the concerns about climate change, social injustice and inequality. The first solution is that we could write new hymns, thus avoiding any drawbacks that older hymns might present. However, any hymn text—even a brand-new text—can express an idea that, over the course of time, turns out to be an idea we feel that we must reject. But of course, a hymn, whether modern or not, may express an unacceptable idea that we sing nevertheless, because we have not thought about its true meaning and have been swept away by a stirring tune. C. S. Lewis, in *The Four Loves,* writes of language:

> Of course language is not an infallible guide,
> but it contains, with all its defects, a good deal

> of stored insight and experience. If you begin by
> flouting it, it has a way of avenging itself later on.[4]

Let us not forget that, when we frown on the prejudices
preserved in older hymns and feel inclined to castigate
their authors, we need to cast a critical eye over the
sentiments expressed in our new hymns. A second
solution to our problem is to revisit older hymns and
revise or adapt them to suit contemporary sensibilities.

We shall be looking at both of these approaches in
detail later. For now, though, we shall explore how
vintage hymns can show the way towards a creative
response to contemporary problems. One way to
confront these is through meditation and reflection
on the words of a well-loved hymn. This may result
in an experience quite different from singing a hymn,
yet contemplating a well-loved hymn such as "When I
survey the wondrous Cross" (Isaac Watts, 1674–1748)
can be, for some, a source of great comfort. Another
way to respond to our difficulties is to take collective
action and band together to confront threats. When we
feel moved to act with others, singing hymns can bolster
our sense of solidarity. In these situations, it is vital that
everyone knows the words which will serve to unite
them in a common purpose. More recent vintage hymns
such as "When I needed a neighbour" (Sydney Carter,
1915–2004) can send out a strong message of Christian
love and charity. However we choose to respond, when
we look with fresh eyes at age-old problems we can find,

in vintage hymns, something to fire the imagination and prompt us to action, each in our own way.

Many hymns from the pre-digital age dwell on the beauties of the natural world and Romantics, such as William Wordsworth (1770–1850), have taught us that natural things are not just beautiful, but have the power to express moral truths which we ignore at our peril. Since the spread of the Romantic ideal, it has been agreed more widely that time spent out-of-doors is time well spent. In "The tables turned" (1798), Wordsworth encourages us to quit the grind of desk-bound work, and seek refreshment outside:

> Up! up! my Friend, and quit your books;
> Or surely you'll grow double:
> Up! up! my Friend, and clear your looks;
> Why all this toil and trouble?

Admiration for the countryside in all its variety is a theme perfectly exemplified in "Glad that I live am I" (Lizette Woodworth Reese, 1856–1935). This joyful hymn appeared in several hymnbooks between 1931 and 1991 but has now fallen from favour with its seemingly dated outlook. Whilst Reese could not possibly have foreseen the kind of disaster faced by future generations such as the COVID-19 pandemic, is it not appropriate that a text which encourages us to celebrate life itself should continue to be sung? Amidst the frustrations of forced isolation and inactivity, the feeling has grown that there might be a welcome opportunity to press the pause button on our hectic daily lives and slow down. We do not know what the future holds for us and must look for comfort where we can. Perhaps vintage hymns can help us through the dark times?

> All that we need to do,
> be we low or high,
> is to see that we grow,
> nearer the sky.

Lost hymns, lost words?

As we consider our natural environment, it is but a small step to the matter of our planet's limited resources which are being eroded through human action. How can vintage hymns help us respond to this emergency? A vital part of being able to perceive our environment in all its infinite detail and wonderful variety is to possess the necessary wealth of vocabulary with which to describe it. We have already seen that many of the hymns we love to sing we learned as children, and many hymns written for children are about nature. Sadly, there has been a trend to eradicate certain words from our language—even among those editing a children's dictionary. Part of education is acquiring such a vocabulary, and this applies to adults and children alike—without words we can have no perception. By impoverishing our vocabulary, however, especially the vocabulary of children, who are of an age to be most receptive to fresh ideas, we undermine our ability to attain a clear perception of nature. In 2017, author Robert Macfarlane drew attention to the fact that certain words in nature are simply disappearing due to lack of use. He writes:

> Once upon a time, words began to vanish from the language of children. They disappeared so quietly that at first almost no one noticed . . . [5]

In his beautiful book *The Lost Words*, exquisitely illustrated by Jackie Morris, Macfarlane recovers some of these lost words—words that are familiar to adults such as heron, bluebell and kingfisher—and brings them back to life with a vibrancy of colour and language. Singing vintage hymns is one way that we can keep these lost words in our vocabulary. In "All things bright and beautiful", for example, Mrs Alexander reminds us of the "glowing colours" which surround us and, I fear, if our attention is no longer drawn to them, we might cease to notice them. We can see the palette of our hymnody becoming grey as we discard other hymns, including "I love God's tiny creatures" (George Wallace Briggs, 1875–1959), which gives us the visually brilliant "coral-coated ladybird" alongside a tactile awareness of the "velvet humming-bee". Another text which emphasizes the light and colour of the natural world is "Daisies are our silver, buttercups are gold" (Jan Struther, 1901–53) which uses the imagery of jewellery and wealth. If the trend to root out unfamiliar words continues, there is a danger that children may come to lack the necessary tools to develop a true appreciation of nature and will grow up caring nothing for the natural world. Would it not be terrible if Bunty Newport's (1927–2004) dystopian hymn "Think of a world without any flowers" actually came true?

Without a doubt singing hymns is one tool that can help draw attention to things of vital importance that we might be in danger of forgetting. As we appreciate the wonders of nature and are spurred to preserve it, our realization that we are dependent on the world around us is sharpened. The ritual of the harvest festival, with its associated vintage hymns, serves to remind us of our total dependence on the fruits of the earth. This annual celebration of God as creator has long been marked by decorating churches, the distribution of produce and the singing of specific hymns including "We plough the fields, and scatter", translated from the German by Jane Montgomery Campbell (1817–78). In more recent years, collection of foodstuff has, rightly, focused on dried and tinned items which are later contributed to a local foodbank or charity. Naturally these longer-lasting provisions are needed by far too many people, but we should remember where our food comes from, and hymns can help us do that. "We plough the fields, and scatter" is a favourite harvest hymn which shows God as artist-creator and provider. Full of sumptuous vocabulary, it is a hymn which cannot fail to lift the heart. Even so harvest festivals are not the full-scale celebrations they once were with their array of overgrown marrows and maggot-infested windfall apples. Could this be because we care so little about where our food comes from? It is universally acknowledged that a tomato plucked from our own crop is sweeter than any bought in a supermarket, but what about the parlous state of food production in the twenty-first century? A damning report published in February 2019 stated that the world's capacity to produce food is being undermined by humanity's failure to protect biodiversity and a readiness to rely on single food crops. We have not learned from history and fail to remember the catastrophic potato famine in Ireland brought about by reliance on a single food crop. "We plough the fields, and scatter" is all too often considered irrelevant to modern life but perhaps singing it could go some way towards keeping this vital topic at the top of our agenda. Another harvest favourite is "Come, ye thankful people, come" by Henry Alford (1810–71). This is a text which links the ripeness of the earthly harvest with our own willingness to serve as workers for God as in Matthew 9:37. Some of the more obscure words of the original text have been dropped in more recent hymnbooks, but the central image of the ripening corn remains. These are just two examples of many which demonstrate that our older hymns have messages to which we can respond and may help us move to decisive action.

Changing words, same belief?

But, I hear you say, the world is changing—and I concur. There are certainly few people in the West who are not touched by innovation which has made our lives both more simple and more complicated. Just as we have seen that we need vocabulary to perceive accurately our natural world, we also need words in order to grasp the rapid rate of change in this technological world. This pace of change has proved problematic for our hymn writers as, in a bid to keep them relevant, valuable texts are rashly discarded and altered—only to discover that the "updated" version itself quickly becomes obsolete. Let's look again at "We plough the fields, and scatter". In 1969, Brian Wren (b. 1936) presented a text which he described as "after Jane Montgomery Campbell". This hymn opens with the line "We plough and sow with tractors" and goes on to mention more modern farm machinery than is referred to in Campbell's original. The transformation that this text has undergone presents an instructive example of how a new text can cause us difficulties of a different kind. It was less than twenty years later when Brian Wren himself felt that he must revisit the text in order to alter all the gender-specific pronouns in keeping with his emerging strict personal policy. I shall return to the topic of gender in hymns later.

So, even a text that we might regard as modern may become outmoded and thus be deemed irrelevant. The difficulty here is that, if texts featuring outmoded references are discarded out of hand, we are in danger of failing to take notice of the social and environmental problems to which they referred that still plague us. One interesting example is "Milk bottle tops and paper bags" (Peggy Blakeley, 1921–2006). This is a children's hymn which confronts the scourge of littering. It appears in only two hymnbooks and is now rarely sung. Could this relative neglect result from the fact that glass milk bottles with their foil tops are largely a thing of the past? Perhaps only older singers will recognize that milk bottle tops have a dual significance. Certainly they are a nuisance as they are a source of litter, but they can also be a valuable resource if collected for charity. This use may well now be considered a quaint activity and may even rank with the gathering rushes of "All things bright and beautiful". Yet fly-tippers are still blighting our countryside and towns now more than ever. Are we not now in need of a hymn like this to alert us to the terrible damage that is being done to our countryside?

> Help us, Lord, to find each day
> ways to help to keep away
> that litter off the pavement,
> that rubbish off the beach.
> For this is what we
> CLAP CLAP CLAP CLAP
> really want to see.
> CLAP CLAP CLAP CLAP
> Yes! Yes! Yes![6]

As we hurry to embrace the latest technological innovations, it is difficult for our hymns to keep up. It may seem that "God of concrete, God of steel" (Richard Jones, b. 1926) is no longer relevant as it conjures up images of a disappearing manufacturing industry. However, as we sing through the hymn, we realize that the true theme is not fast-changing technological advances, but a reminder that as creator, God is constant:

> God whose glory fills the earth
> gave the universe its birth
> loosed the Christ with Easter's might
> saves the world from evil's blight
> claims mankind by grace divine
> all the world of love is thine.

Or as Percy Dearmer (1867–1936) puts it in his paraphrase of Goethe's text, "Everything changes, but God changes not". There is a suspicion that if we allow ourselves to sing seemingly dated hymns, we are betraying an inability to make sense of the modern world. However, I would argue that social ills do not vanish just because the reference in a hymn is regarded as out of date. The inequalities Fred Kaan (1929–2009) wrote about in "Sing we a song of high revolt" in the 1960s are just as widespread today, even though the "council flats" have been taken over by housing associations or private ownership. If texts such as these are discarded out of hand, we are in danger of forgetting what we so need to remember. Perhaps it would be better to continue to sing hymns such as these—even with their obsolete references—if only to remind us of problems which plague us to this very day. Whichever course we take, we need to keep these urgent concerns in our hearts and minds.

The world is facing grave problems from social inequality and external threats such as climate change. Whilst there is a tendency to seek political and technological solutions to these difficulties, many are the result of the selfish actions of individuals. It is easy to ask for change, but difficult to effect this unless it comes from the heart and within. One important way that change of heart can be brought about is through communal activities, one of which is singing hymns. We have already argued that hymn singing can engage our emotions and imagination in a way that can lead to a new understanding and even prompt affirmative action. Although not originally written as a hymn, "Jerusalem" is a text which opens our minds to possibility and aspiration. Of course, it has complex associations. It is remembered as a rallying call to the public in the midst of the First World War and has long been associated with victories on the battlefield, as well as the supremacy of the British Empire. Rarely sung in churches now, except in the occasional civic service, "Jerusalem" has a reputation for being enjoyed by the flag-waving masses for whom any unease is quickly swept away by the desire to have a good time. However, in the text Blake sets out a vision of a land free of inequality—and indeed a New Jerusalem suitable as a resting place for the Son of God himself. When considered from this point of view, it seems completely appropriate that it should have been adopted in 1918 by the women's suffrage movement. Even today the hymn remains the unofficial anthem of the Women's Institute (WI). Although this movement is sometimes ridiculed, it is an organization which lobbies for positive change in society—and perhaps through its unobtrusive activities is playing its part in realizing Blake's vision of the "green and pleasant land". Could it be that the search for solutions to some of the world's current problems might lie within ourselves rather than in political and technological "fixes"? Change is happening for the better in the lives of many women—albeit far too slowly—and can we say that perhaps, just perhaps, the singing of "Jerusalem" by the WI has assisted this? Blake's poem, now a vintage hymn, can certainly fuel our imagination and, through the power of his vision, his work has a capacity to stir us to action. Another vintage hymn which bids us follow the Christian path amongst the evils of society is John Bunyan's "Who would true valour see". A text which, again, did not start life as a hymn has had a rocky ride over the last hundred years with the hobgoblins and foul fiends of the third verse in the original falling in and out of favour. Even so, it serves to demonstrate how a hymn can be familiar and loved in several different versions.

In our quest to keep our hymns relevant, we have already acknowledged that we want to hold on to beautiful language which fuels our imagination. Like "Jerusalem", "Who would true valour see" is rooted firmly in our literary culture, coming as it does from John Bunyan's *Pilgrim's Progress* (1678). The story, of course, is allegorical but few would dispute that nothing is more likely to stir our imaginations. Yet there have been, historically, some problems with taking the text directly from the book and including it for congregational singing. The text appears as "He who would valiant be" for the first time in the *English Hymnal* (1906). Percy Dearmer, the hymnbook's general editor, explains in *Songs of Praise Discussed* that the aim was to meet a desire to include cheerful—and bizarrely—"manly" hymns. However, he felt that it would be unacceptable for Christians in the twentieth century to sing the word "hobgoblin" on the grounds that the word does not appear in the Bible. This seems a weak point as the Bible is a translation and so no English words appear in it! Declaring that it would "ensure disaster" to include these mythical creatures, nevertheless he remains content to keep the giants of the first verse on the grounds that giants are mentioned in the Bible.[7] Musing on this point, I conclude that Dearmer subscribed to the belief that God is surely an Englishman, and, accordingly, the Bible should have been written in English. As the Padre thought, in J. G. Farrell's *The Siege of Krishnapur*:

> He could not understand why the Bible should
> have had to be translated at all, even in the
> first place . . . why it should have been written
> in Hebrew and Greek when English was the
> obvious language . . . English was spoken in
> every corner of every continent.[8]

However, if there is any place where a language that
feeds our imagination it is in our hymns, irrespective of
whether those specific words are found in the Bible (or
its translations) or not. Thankfully, our hobgoblins have
been given a more friendly welcome in other published
hymnbooks, thus ensuring that the language of
imagination remains alive and well in our hymn-singing
tradition. Furthermore, it cannot go unnoticed that it
was Percy Dearmer who commissioned Jan Struther to
write "When a knight won his spurs" with its reference to
dragons, knights and storyland—all possibly biblically
suspect! This hymn, written to fit the tune STOWEY in
Songs of Praise, is now rarely sung, although it is in many
hymnbooks, including some of the more recent ones.
The language of medieval battles complete with armour
and coupled with virtues of gallantry and valour may
seem to have little place in our lives today. Yet do not
modern computer games encourage us to triumph over
mythical beasts? And in our lives, are we not encouraged
to "tame our inner dragons"?

Before leaving "Who would true valour see", I would
like to explore some more of the ideas which render a

hymn relevant or not. We will be exploring the use of gender-specific language in detail later on, but it is worth pausing to consider how deeply embedded in hymns is the idea of masculine superiority. Dearmer's desire to set down a "manly" hymn does not sit comfortably with many singers today. He changes the first line from "Who would true valour see" to "He who would valiant be", which may seem to some an aggressive use of a masculine pronoun. In Dearmer's favour, though, he changes the constant use of "he" in the original to "I" in the first verse. How then can hymnbook editors respond to this controversial use of gender-specific language? Well, they could simply change the first line of the hymn. Exactly this was done by the publisher Kevin Mayhew towards the end of the twentieth century when the opening line became "All who would valiant be". This creates an unforeseen difficulty, however, with this much-loved vintage hymn—we can't find it in the hymnbook! This may seem a trivial point, but it could have serious consequences. Once the first line—indeed the first word—of a hymn is changed, there is a danger it will get lost, especially if, as in the case of the Kevin Mayhew hymnbooks, the texts are arranged alphabetically. So, on balance, then, if we want to preserve this vintage hymn, it could be said that using Dearmer's first line is preferable to using Kevin Mayhew's.

In Dearmer's "He who would valiant be", we find an anxious hymnbook editor who has chosen to reject aspects of a text for reasons of caution. Retaining or rejecting hobgoblins may seem unimportant, but what about when it comes to accepting or rejecting whole ideologies? We have already seen that the collective act of hymn singing serves to join us together as a community and at best hymns have the ability to stir us to action and respond to social and environmental matters. Hymns, then, have the ability to shape the way that singers both see themselves and, potentially, the way they live their lives. It is clear that whilst hymns may have something admirable to say, it would be naïve to accept that all older hymns are suitable for singing today. Are these hymns "old-fashioned" or "vintage"? This is the question we shall ask as we consider the reasons which weigh with us when we think about why a hymn is no longer relevant.

Is God an Englishman?

One of the reasons why a hymn may no longer be considered relevant is because it is associated with patriotism and the British Empire—ideas to which we may no longer wish to subscribe. In the summer of 2020, there raged a fierce debate about the inclusion of certain texts in the *Last Night of the Proms* programme with strong opinions voiced on either side. At its most basic, the two opposing factions were divided between "tradition" (i.e. we have always done it this way) and the desire for change (i.e. these texts are no longer appropriate). It is easy to see in our older hymnbooks that God favoured Britain over other nations! The very existence of "national" sections in some collections is testament to this and the expression of patriotic fervour appears again and again especially in Victorian hymns— many of which continue to be sung today. Although a sentiment that was strongest when the Empire was at its height, there is earlier evidence of this attitude. Isaac Watts (1674–1748), for example, in his versification of the *Psalms of David in the Language of the New Testament* (1719), suggested that the British people were favoured by God above all others in return for their righteous living. Psalm 104:12 reads:

> O bless his Name, ye Britons, fed
> With Nature's chief supporter, bread;
> While bread you vital strength imparts,
> Serve him with vigour in your hearts.

While Britons were called upon to live pious lives and to ensure they were worthy of the honour and power bestowed upon them, their superiority over other nations was without question. In "God of our father, known of old" by Rudyard Kipling (1865–1936), there is a clear warning that any loss of self-control would result in behaviour typical of "lesser breeds". Clearly many singers today will find this stance unacceptable and the text has not been included in a hymnbook since 1960. This is surely significant as it was this year when many

African nations were granted independence. That with power comes responsibility is clear, but the implication that authority and wisdom have been granted to a single country—called either the "fatherland" (e.g. "To thee our God we fly" (W. W. How, 1823–97)) or the "motherland" (as in the Kipling text noted above)—may strike many singers as absurd and offensive. The text by How, though, has limped on into the twenty-first century and is included in *Complete Anglican Hymns Old & New*.

Of course "The Empire" as it was in Victoria's reign has ceased to exist and for this reason many of the hymns that are associated with it have faded from our consciousness and disappeared from many of our hymnbooks. Before sweeping aside hymns that are no longer considered relevant, it is worth remembering that such texts were, in their day, well-known and well-loved. How do we know this? Once more we can look to novels to see how the knowledge of such hymns extends well beyond the church pew. In Paul Scott's *The Raj Quartet*, a four-volume novel teeming with local colour, sexual intrigue and political struggle set in the Second World War, there are several occasions when hymns are sung. Scott makes a point of telling us that they come from *Hymns Ancient & Modern, New Standard* (1922). This is a hymnbook that English singers would almost certainly have known from their schools and parish churches, and it is easy to imagine that the familiarity of the volume would provide these singers with something of a bridge to take them home—metaphorically at least. In *The*

Raj Quartet, the tensions between English and Indian, army and mission are never far away with colour, class, money and education all very much in evidence. Church services—all conducted in an Anglican church—observe a rigid structure, both liturgical and social, and there was often some difficulty as to who would sit where! The first church service mentioned in the book is an officer's funeral which, of course, reminds us that it is the men who are fighting and dying while the women wait at home. No surprise then, that the first hymn is Somerset Thomas Corry Lowry's (1855–1932) "Lord, while afar our brothers fight". The text makes clear that the cost, in human terms, is high and that those in battle "may nevermore return again". There is no question of defeat as God was always, in their minds at least, on the side of the British. However, it is worth remembering that the stakes were high. Not only were the men involved in a war, but the women were in a foreign country facing a terrible threat and an uncertain future. Is it not understandable, then, that they should want to cling to any small piece of home—even if it is only a hymnbook?

Intimately connected with the presence of the British in India was the work of missionaries. The tension between army and mission school with its work of education and conversion is central to *The Raj Quartet*. When we think about the hymns associated with mission, we encounter hymns that we may want both to keep and reject simultaneously. One of the most popular hymns of the missionary movement is "From

Greenland's icy mountains", a hymn which we have already noted for its quality of language. Throughout the text we have glimpses of different regions of the world, each vividly described. The hymn begins:

> From Greenland's icy mountains
> from India's coral strand,
> where Afric's sunny fountains
> roll down their golden sand,
> from many ancient rivers,
> from many a palmy plain . . .

Despite this rich use of exotic imagery however, the paean to English virility and superiority gives us pause.

> Can we, whose souls are lighted
> with wisdom from on high,
> can we to men benighted
> the lamp of life deny?
> Salvation! O salvation!
> the joyful sound proclaim,
> till each remotest nation
> has learned Messiah's name.

With its reference to the so-called "civilizing mission", it would seem that even Paul Scott felt some unease with the text when he writes:

> everyone knew [it] and could sing happily
> without bothering much about the words.[9]

Heber's hymn was largely dropped from hymnbooks after the middle of the twentieth century, but, perhaps not surprisingly, it appears in *Redemption Songs*. Here, then, is a classic case where we are torn in two directions. Do we keep this hymn for its beauty of language and because of the reputation of the writer, or reject it on the grounds of its assumption of Christian superiority?

Missionary hymns were written for children who sang them at school in England and thereby were made aware of their responsibility to spread the Good News to the heathen races. The repellently patronizing hymn "Over the seas there are little brown children" (Hetty Lee, 1878–1954) mercifully appeared in only one hymnbook, *Sunday School Praise*, although it is to my shame that I know all the words by heart!

> Over the seas there are little brown children,
> Fathers and mothers and babies dear;
> They have not heard of the Father in heaven,
> No one has told them that God is near.
>
> *Swift let the message go over the water,*
> *Telling the children that God is near.*
>
> Sometimes at night when the darkness gathers,
> Little brown children begin to fear;
> They have not heard of the Father in heaven,
> No one has told them that God is near.

Little brown children, the teachers are coming,
speeding to love you, and help, and cheer;
soon you shall hear of the dear Lord Jesus
Soon they will tell you that God is near.

Where is the battle front?

Another feature of hymns which may render them
"old-fashioned" rather than "vintage" is the attitude that
they express towards warfare. The two central ideas to
consider are, first, that of a literal battle and, second, that
of a spiritual battle. However, the way in which singers
choose to respond to this call to arms will govern their
interpretation. Hymns often contain military images,
but this can leave us uncertain as to whether such images
refer to spiritual struggles or conflict on the battlefield.
It is difficult to disentangle these two interpretations
and sometimes a text has been used to fire our military
ardour even if the author intended it to refer to a purely
spiritual struggle. Texts such as "Soldiers of the cross,
arise" (W. W. How), for example, lend themselves to
stiffening morale while justifying an earthly war with
the rather different aim of establishing the kingdom
of God on earth. "Onward Christian Soldiers" (Sabine
Baring-Gould, 1834–1924) is probably the most widely
known of such hymns. Set to the rousing tune ST
GERTRUDE (Arthur Sullivan, 1842–1900), it is easy to
see how one can be swept away on a wave of evangelical

zeal which could all too easily descend into a lust for battle. Although written for a Sunday school procession and not for military purposes at all, it is a hymn which pops up on state and civic occasions and even finds a mention in *The Raj Quartet*.

In the twenty-first century, popularity often seems to trump suitability when selecting hymns—with a rousing tune often being the deciding factor. "Stand up, stand up for Jesus" (George Duffield, 1818–88) is one such text—especially when sung to an uplifting tune such as MORNING LIGHT (George James Webb, 1803–87). Whether we interpret "war" as an earthly or a spiritual battle, one can understand how any such hymn could perpetuate the idea that power is in itself a force for good in the world. This hymn appears in countless hymnbooks including the most recent edition of *Mission Praise*. It may seem reasonable, on the face of it, that hymns that could be interpreted as supporting war should no longer be sung. However, it remains the case that there is conflict in the world and singers will need to work out their response to this. One response is to reject the whole idea of warfare and when such a hymn is sung it will be understood that it is a spiritual battle that is raging. Of course, there will be singers who believe that there are some wars that are just. In their case, the moral question arises over whether the war is conducted with honour. It is for the individual to decide and, either way, these vintage hymns can, perhaps, go some way towards offering some personal resolution, whatever that may be.

The strong association with the military is but one of the many instances in which gender stereotyping has come under scrutiny in hymns. It is only in the latter half of the twentieth century that patriarchy in the Church has been widely challenged. We have already seen in our examination of hymns which use military language and imagery that it is men who are seen as uniquely suited to the tough life of a soldier equipped for the responsibilities of leadership on the battlefield, while women are seen as passive bystanders wringing their hands. As Somerset Corry Lowry put it:

> For wives and mothers sore distress'd
> For all who wait in silent fear,
> For homes bereaved which gave their best,
> For hearts now desolate and drear,
> O God of comfort, hear our cry,
> and in the darkest hour draw nigh.

The strength of the male is often contrasted with the meekness and frailty of the female—qualities which, according to Brian Wren, are "downgraded or despised".[10] Without doubt the subject of gender inclusivity in hymn texts is large, and we shall be looking at it in more detail later on. For now, though, it is worth pausing to consider how all too often the use of masculine-specific language is used in connection with winning the battle for salvation. Typical is Edward H. Bickersteth's (1825–1906) "O brothers, lift your voices", which is full of the language of conflict with the spoils of war metaphors for spiritual successes:

> Faith is our battle-token;
> Our leader all controls:
> Our trophies, fetters broken;
> Our captives, ransomed souls.

Throughout the text the conquerors are always brothers or brethren and although it may seem of little importance to include only men in the fight for the kingdom, many find it difficult to justify singing a text which completely excludes fifty percent of the population! Even so, our task here is not to favour one side of this argument over the other, but to identify texts which remain relevant and speak to us today. We know that singers will sing the hymns they want to sing! In order to make these hymns relevant, texts may be altered and updated, and it is this that we will consider next.

CHAPTER 3

Altering texts

Tinkering or tweaking?

Deciding whether a text is relevant to our current needs is by no means straightforward and may rest on a number of factors weighing either in favour or against the same hymn. We have seen that hymns have been altered—and indeed are being altered—to suit changing needs, opinions and sensibilities. The power of a hymn, as we have noted, extends far beyond the church pew, which leads us to the crucial question: Can we alter a hymn without destroying its power?

The changes that can be made to a hymn text can take many different forms, and it will always be a moot point whether this or that change really alters the "content" or the "flavour" of the hymn. There is a whole spectrum of possible alterations to a text that may strike different people in different ways. Nevertheless, it may be helpful to provide some rules of thumb to help us examine the various kinds of change a hymn text can undergo. The smallest kind of change—which we might call "tinkering"—is to replace a word or words with an exact equivalent that will leave the overall meaning or content of the hymn text unaltered. The kind of changes I have in mind here are replacing more archaic words such as "thee" and "thine" with "you" and "yours" and so forth. Of course, what will be regarded by one person as an "exact" equivalent may not be accepted as such by another. So, even at this microscopic level, agreement is far from assured. The second kind of change—which we might call "tweaking"—is when more significant alterations are made, although such changes in the wording leave the basic content of the hymn intact. These may include altering masculine and feminine pronouns. Although attention is paid to maintaining the feel of text, this can wrong-foot many singers. A striking example is the well-known Christmas hymn "God rest ye merry, gentlemen", which in some newer hymnbooks has been altered to "God rest you merry, gentlefolk" (whoever they may be!). Perhaps, some might argue, this piece of tweaking, whilst undeniably gender-inclusive, renders the text puzzlingly unfamiliar. The third kind of alteration is "rewriting" when more substantial portions of the hymn are modified. This frequently changes the "flavour" or "feel" of the text, and we can lose some of the beauties of language that led us to treasure this vintage hymn in the first place. Finally, the fourth kind of alteration is where a vintage text is adapted to become part of a longer hymn which may involve extensive revision and a new tune.

Why alter texts?

Now we shall consider these changes in more detail and examine what impact they have on our vintage hymns. Some may claim that we should eliminate all non-contemporary language from our hymns, which would include altering the pronouns and remodelling archaic sentence structures. Certainly it would bring our hymns up to date and in this sense make them more relevant—but what effect does this have on our hymn-singing tradition? This kind of change, at least, has the value of consistency since church liturgy has also undergone many revisions over the centuries in order to introduce more modern modes of speech in services. The most obvious is using the vernacular instead of Latin and our hymns have followed suit. It is rare, for example, for congregations and informal groups to sing in Latin from the pew. Yet "Puer nobis nascitur", a hymn from various medieval sources, appears in many collections as the vintage Christmas hymn "Unto us a boy is born". Some might argue that these ancient Latin texts are an essential part of our hymn-singing tradition—but if a text cannot be understood by large sections of the community, can it count as a tradition? We also use new Bible translations and modify ancient prayers, so why not change old hymns in the same way? This brings us directly to one of the essential components of our hymn-singing tradition—that of inclusivity.

Before considering substantial changes to texts, I want to think about the small changes—the "tinkering". This might mean quietly exchanging a "thee" for a "you", or a "dost" for a "do". Harmless enough, one might think—but enough of a change to bring you up short when you are trying to sing along. More important than the general feeling among singers that they want to continue with the words they know and love, these small changes can make it difficult for people to continue singing their favourite hymns. Studies have shown that the elderly, especially those suffering from dementia, can continue joining in with the hymns they love long after other cognitive faculties have failed. Surely these people have just as much right to enjoy their hymns as any other singer? Even minor tinkering with texts can frustrate singers and does not necessarily result in a more accessible text. In addition, it is worth saying that many groups of singers can happily sing archaic words especially if they feel that it is part of a tradition they want to maintain. Why, for example, sing "O come, all you faithful" when "O come, all ye faithful" has sufficed for over one hundred years? It seems strange to update some pronouns, then leave difficult—even incomprehensible—words in a new translation. *Mission Praise 30th Anniversary Version* contains various adjustments to this hymn, but still contains the line "He, who abhors not the virgin's womb", which to my mind is the most difficult line in the whole hymn—and fails what I call "the body parts test", too, as we shall see! Small grammatical changes also bring little benefit. "Lord, thy word abideth" (Henry W. Baker, 1821–77) is a case in point. The hymn was written for *Hymns Ancient & Modern* (1861) and is faithfully reproduced in many collections including *Mission Praise 30th Anniversary Edition*. It is a popular hymn, and whilst perhaps not in the top ten, it is known and loved by many. Strange then that it should take on a new life as "Lord, your word abiding" in a few hymnbooks in the second half of the twentieth century. There is no doubt that the words have been brought up to date, but it is harder to sing multiple "ing"s than lots of "eth"s. Some singers may also feel that if we adjust these more archaic expressions, we may lose something of the essential quality of the hymn.

Our hymns have been evolving in parallel with liturgical language all along. Aside from the fact that we now generally sing hymns in our own language, hymns deemed new are, indeed, some of our finest vintage hymns. For example, "Lord of all hopefulness, Lord of all joy" (Jan Struther) was one of the first hymns to use "you" when addressing the son of God. It remains a firm favourite in schools, church services, and at weddings and funerals. Although it has the feel of a recent hymn, it was included in many twentieth-century hymnbooks right back to the 1930s and so has certainly earned its spurs as a vintage hymn. Aside from the newer hymns incorporating contemporary words and turns of phrase, changes have gradually been made to older texts. However, it is an illusion to think that the versions of texts we know and love have never undergone previous revision. Far from being set in stone, they have already been changed many times at the recommendation of hymnbook editors or even the authors themselves. A much-cited example of this is "Hark! The herald-angels sing". Charles Wesley's famous text started life in 1739 as "Hark, how all the welkin rings", although he altered it himself and published the new version in his own *Hymns and Sacred Poems* (1743). The later version has been reproduced in countless hymnbooks. The earlier version was published in *Songs of Praise* and *The English Hymnal (New Edition)* (1933), where it appears alongside the newer version. This in itself is interesting as Percy Dearmer, general editor of both books and master of inconsistency, was happy to keep the "welkin" version, although it is an unusual word—and definitely not in the Bible! It was as unlikely to be known to singers in the 1930s as it is to singers today. The old version makes a later appearance in *Carols Old and New* presumably to satisfy the "Old" element in the title of the collection. That being so, it is unlikely that the older words would be used by carol singers in the community today. Whilst the "old" version may be sung for historical reasons by a choir, the "new" version has become the accepted version and is sung at Christmas celebrations every year.

Same word, several meanings

There may be a desire to exclude certain words because (it is claimed) they have changed their meaning. A curious form of censorship has crept in with what I call the "body parts" test being strictly applied. Words such as "bowels", "bosom" and "breast" are often frowned upon—perhaps as a result of a giggling reception from the Year 9s? An illuminating example is "In the bleak mid-winter" (Christina Rossetti, 1830–94), which contains that most maternal of images, "a breastful of milk". The focus of this carol is frequently the last verse, "What can I give him, poor as I am?" as a reminder of the unworthiness of us all to come into the presence of the infant king, but it still seems, to me, a shame that the breast-feeding verse is censored in some versions. Perhaps revulsion at the thought that the Son of Man should require sustenance from his mother? Indeed there is a curious sense of prudishness in contemporary hymn versions which surpasses even that of the Victorians! It seems that anything goes rather than mention what are clearly thought of as the naughty bits. There are many instances of this, including "Jesu, lover of my soul" (Charles Wesley), which surely enjoys prime place in our hymn-singing tradition, yet the "bosom" of the second line has been altered to "presence" and "comfort" in some more recent versions.

There is no doubt that many of our older hymns use a vocabulary which may appear at best outdated and at worst offensive. The meanings of some words, of course, have evolved and finding them in an older text can be disconcerting. The word "gay" for example has previously been used to mean joyous and happy. A useful word when writing verse because it rhymes with "play", as in "All hail, ye little martyr flowers" (Athelstan L. Riley, 1868–1945), it features in many earlier texts for children:

> First victims of the Martyr bands,
> with crown and palms in tender hands,
> around the very altar, gay
> and innocent, ye seem to play.

However, as the word acquired an additional sense, especially for the LGBT community, it has become more unusual to sing hymns using it. Gaiety in the sense of happiness is found in many traditional hymns, and it would be a shame to lose hymns such as "Daisies are our silver, buttercups our gold"—a hymn I have already praised for its rich language—on the grounds that the "leaves in April" are "gay". In some contemporary hymns, the word "gay" is used to emphasize that the love of God is not limited by a person's sexual orientation. Bold new texts such as Andrew Pratt's "There are no limits to God's love" and Brian Wren's "Come, welcome Christ in every face" both contrast "gay" with "straight" and are examples of how it is possible to absorb a change of meaning into our hymns. When a word acquires a new sense, we should not allow it to colour our understanding of the same word as it appears in any earlier hymns.

There is a continuing debate about whether to keep older literature on the school curriculum. Many question the value of forcing students to grapple with archaic language found in the works of authors like Chaucer or Shakespeare. This is not the place to try to settle this question, but it remains a fact that these older authors remain on the syllabus because many believe that young people should have the opportunity to sample their use of language—archaic as it might be—because it will deepen their understanding of the English language itself. In other words, the archaic language, far from being a drawback, is one of the many reasons for studying older authors. If there is any truth in this, is it not strange that we should fail to value vintage hymns for their language, too? They should be prized as a source of enrichment and not eliminated from the repertoire. Language is always changing. If singers can happily join in with "wanna" and "gonna", is a "wouldst" and "couldst" really going to cause such a problem? We need to think carefully before eradicating older words which deepen our understanding and stir our imagination. Take "O thou who camest from above" (Charles Wesley), for example. Here is a hymn which would appear to break all the contemporary language rules. It contains archaic structures, long words—of which "inextinguishable" is the longest. It also contains at least one word—namely "mean"—that has acquired a new sense in recent times:

> Kindle a flame of sacred love
> on the mean altar of my heart.

This hymn, though, appears to have survived as it is in many published hymnbooks including those of the twenty-first century. The inclusion of Wesley's beautiful text in some of our more recent hymnbooks shows that there are treasures among our hymns which we would be foolish to discard.

Hymns or hers?

A further significant alteration to hymn texts concerns gender inclusivity and stereotyping. For brevity, let us use the term "gender pronoun" for any word that implies that the people referred to have a definite gender. The use of gender pronouns is not an objectionable practice in itself. For example, no one will object to using "he" to refer to St Peter or "she" to refer to St Cecilia. There is universal agreement that, in these cases, the relevant pronouns refer to people whose gender is not under debate. One difficulty arises when a gender pronoun is used to refer to a person whose gender is unknown. The problem is that English does not possess a pronoun for referring to a person of unknown gender. "It" is not used to refer to a person except in a derogatory way. Therefore, the tradition has been to use the word "he" for want of a better word. This practice can cause offence—hence the growing trend for using plurals—"they", "them" and "their" to refer to people of unknown gender. This, as we shall see, can cause some headaches for hymn writers and editors. Even more problematic is the use of strictly inappropriate gender words to refer to one or more persons whose gender is known. Using "brothers" and "brethren" to refer to a group of people that certainly contains women is highly objectionable to many.

However, not all attempts to correct gender bias lead to the improvement intended. James Phillip McAuley's (1917–76) text, for example, after a unison refrain, which opens with the line "Men are the sons of God and therefore brothers", has been variously rewritten with some odd results. The original appears in *With One Voice*, yet in *Baptist Praise and Worship* the fault is compounded as the line is "improved" to "We are the sons of God, sister and brother"! Mercifully in *Hymns & Psalms* the line appears as "Sisters and brothers are we as God's children".

In our hymns, the words "man" and "mankind" are particularly difficult. Originally, the words "man" and "men" did not necessarily refer to males, but to any human being, male or female. Although the words have retained something of this sense in some contexts, they have become used much more often as a way of referring to males, as opposed to females. Now that these words are predominantly used to refer to men and boys, the use of "man" and "mankind" to refer to people in general can cause offence. As there are many hundreds of hymn texts which contain the word "mankind" referring to the whole of humanity, altering them all would, of course, be a mammoth undertaking. Furthermore, we come up against our old dilemma that we may both wish to discard and retain the very same text. There is, though, an argument that gender-specific—even misogynistic—language should be allowed to remain if the text is considered historically important. Some people, though, would dispute the validity of this line of argument. An example of this is Thomas Carlyle's (1795–1881) translation of Martin Luther's "A safe stronghold our God is still". This hymn contains a verse that suggests that wives and children are mere possessions and assigns a role to women that implies an unfavourable comparison with men:

> And though they take our life,
> goods, honour, children, wife,
> yet is their profit small;
> these things shall vanish all:
> the city of God remaineth.

Alarmingly, this text has survived word for word in over forty hymnbooks, the most recent of which is *Mission Praise 30th Anniversary Edition*. Perhaps, I suggest, it is once more the marrying of a text to a well-known and strong tune such as EIN'FESTE BURG that seduces us into overlooking the import of these words. A variant, by Rupert E. Davies (1909–94), which appears in more recent hymnbooks used by the Methodist Church, recasts these lines to read:

> And though before our eyes
> All that we dearly prize
> They seize beyond recall,
> Yet is their profit small
> God's kingdom ours remaineth.

The debate surrounding gender inclusivity has, in more recent decades, extended to questioning the constant reference to God with a specifically masculine pronoun. It would be a very long book indeed that deals exhaustively with the myriad of references to Lord, King and Father in our hymns. Nevertheless, the Christian God has almost always been referred to as male. Since there is no logical reason why God should be regarded as male any more than female, the exclusive use of masculine pronouns in our hymns is liable to cause offence. One simple reason is that there is no pronoun in English for an entity that is like a human being in many crucial respects, but is utterly unlike human beings in other ways. The option of using the neuter pronoun "it" for God does not appeal, because it seems to demote God to the level of an unthinking entity. What then is the answer? If the almost universal

use in hymn texts of masculine pronouns to refer to God
is found unacceptable, then a great many popular and
much-loved hymn texts will need either to be rewritten
or suppressed!

In the second half of the twentieth century, some
attempts have been made to address this difficulty. We
have already looked at Brian Wren's treatment of "We
plough the fields, and scatter"—a text to which we shall
now return. In the earlier version, published in 1969,
Wren, like Campbell before him, starts the second verse
with the line, "He only is the maker". The verse continues
using masculine pronouns throughout and the third
verse makes specific mention of the deity as male. By
1983, Wren had developed his ideas about using male-
dominated gender words and rewrote the verses using
the words "creator", "friend", "partner" and "companion",
thus avoiding the troublesome gender words. Brian
Wren, however, is only one of several more recent
hymn writers who feel the need to update their texts to
incorporate gender-neutral language. Another example
is "For the healing of the nations" written by Fred Kaan
to mark Human Rights Day in 1965. Included in his first
collection of hymns, *Pilgrim Praise*, it was used by his
congregation at the Pilgrim Church, Plymouth, before it
was formally published. It was considered a radical text
for its time, reminding Christians of their obligation
to work for unity rather than to assume it would just
happen. The original version of the text includes male
gender words, language that Kaan was to discard in later

years. For example, the second verse starts "Lead us, Father, into freedom". Gradually, Fred came to believe that the certainty of a male God was unwarranted and changed the line to "Lead us forward into freedom". This is no less urgent, and the line is still addressed to God. Verse 3 in the original has "dogmas keeping man from man" and he changed this to "dogmas that obscure your plan". Although a relatively new hymn to the canon, "For the healing of the nations" is a well-known and much-sung hymn often used at national, international and even state occasions around the world. "For the healing of the nations" has been published in fifty-six hymnbooks since it was written in 1965. This is all well and good, but since many of these books are still in use today, there is no way of preventing the singing of the earlier version of words from which Kaan distanced himself. We must face the fact that once a hymn is published, it is forever available in all its versions—good or bad. Does this really affect the power of the hymn Kaan intended with its central message of unity? In all honesty, probably not. The text continues to be sung in all its versions as a message for peace and the end of war.

A new tradition?

In spite of the difficulties outlined above, on the whole we are happy to continue singing many of the vintage hymns which are known and loved in whatever version they have come down to us. Equally, we have seen that some hymns do not sit easily with us and need either to be altered or jettisoned. The next question that faces us, however, is how much of a text can be changed before the essential quality of that hymn is lost. It is all well and good to stumble over a couple of words in a carol service, but to be presented with a whole new set of words . . . ? Perhaps there are ways we can enjoy singing hymns even when they are altered provided that the core of a given hymn remains constant amid changes, both small and large. After all, it is this central core of a hymn that we know and love.

CHAPTER 4

A new tradition

Old texts, new ideas?

Hymn singing is fluid. Perhaps it is one of the joys of hymn singing that we can keep revisiting and re-evaluating our favourites. Contemporary hymn writers approach this in two ways. The first is that a writer, inspired by the original words, will write a new set of verses in the same metre so that the result can be sung to the same tune. In this instance, it is essential that the new verses are such that singers can recognize at once the relationship to the original. The result is exciting in that it will be both familiar and unfamiliar at the same time. One such example is "O little town of Nazareth" by Chris Avis (b. 1942). Set to the familiar tune FOREST GREEN, the hymn is reminiscent of "O little town of Bethlehem", but focuses on the life of Christ and the message of hope which transcends the simple message of the Christmas story. In this instance, there is a counterpoint between the old text and the new. The original text remains vivid in the mind of the singer, but the new text presents a fresh resonance.

The second way that a vintage hymn is reworked is when a writer takes a familiar hymn and weaves other words—or even complete verses—into it. Once more this allows the singer to join in with familiar words but with the broadening effect of a different point of view. One way of looking at this is to think about a modern interpretation of a classic book on television or in a film. We may be very familiar with the text of, say, Jane Austen's *Emma*, but we can gain new insights into the original through a fresh interpretation in a different medium. A traditional production complete with beautiful costumes and period dialogue is certainly enjoyable, but that is not to say that a less literal version of *Emma*, such as the film *Clueless* (1995), will not reveal something new.

In our hymns, a particularly exciting example of seeing a familiar hymn with fresh eyes is Sue Gilmurray's (b. 1950) reworking of "Away in a manger". In the original, we have a typical Christmas card version of a baby sleeping with the suspiciously well-behaved animals round about. Gilmurray, though, reminds us of a troubled world full of conflict and warring factions— probably as much in evidence two thousand years ago as they are now:

> Away in a manger, no crib for a bed,
> the little Lord Jesus laid down his sweet head;
> the stars in the bright sky looked down where he lay,
> the little Lord Jesus asleep on the hay.

Away from the manger, the King has his way;
his anger and greed give the order to slay.
In power he decides that the blows have to fall,
and death is the lot of the helpless and small.

The cattle are lowing, the baby awakes,
but little Lord Jesus no crying he makes.
I love you, Lord Jesus, look down from the sky
and stay by my side until morning is nigh.

The cattle are lucky! They don't live in fear,
or cry in the night when there's no-one to hear,
or think someone loves them, and
    find they were wrong,
or pay with their pain for the sins of the strong.

We need you, Lord Jesus, in weakness revealed,
to show how the wounds of our world can be healed,
and children and women and men come to know
the worth that we gain from the love you bestow.

Be near me, Lord Jesus, I ask you to stay
close by me for ever, and love me, I pray.
Bless all the dear children in your tender care,
and fit us for heaven, to live with you there.[11]

This text is not published in a mainstream hymnbook
and needs to be hunted out via websites and hymn
resources. It is therefore unlikely that it will be sung

by community carol singers outside a supermarket! Even so, its very existence breathes new life into the traditional Christmas hymn so enjoyed by singers of all ages each Christmas. Gilmurray has composed a new tune to accompany the words as she said herself that it might seem odd for singers to use the familiar tune with her more sober verses. However, the traditional tune used in England, CRADLE SONG (William James Kirkpatrick, 1838–1921) gives the unfamiliar words a particular poignance.

There are plenty of examples of how contemporary singer/songwriters take a text and weave their own words into the original whilst leaving whole sections of the previous hymn intact. Although horrified purists may resist such innovations, the results are extremely popular. One of the best-known examples is Stuart Townend's (b. 1963) "The Lord's my shepherd, I'll not want". This is a reworking of the versification of the twenty-third Psalm by Francis Rous (1579–1659), a vintage hymn if ever there was one! The original has an impressive pedigree. It has been sung on royal and state occasions, as well as at weddings, funerals and remembrance services the world over. Why then, one might ask, do we need another version? Perhaps the answer is that a new version does not replace the old version, but allows those with different musical tastes, who might never otherwise have encountered these fine words, to discover and appreciate them. That Townend's version is published in thirty-one hymnbooks is testament to its popularity. Of course, these reworkings—resulting in what are generally called "Worship Songs"—are sung to completely different tunes which can often rely on a substantial group of musicians to guarantee their success in performance. Although they may be popular in places where a complex electrical set-up is feasible, it is much harder to perform them in intimate or open-air settings—thus for the purposes of singing around a village war memorial the Rous version of "The Lord's my shepherd" may trump Townend's.

The usual suspects?

Our hymn-singing tradition remains vibrant in all its forms whether it is singing a text that resounds across the centuries, enjoying a favourite from school days, reimagining a familiar hymn, or joining in with the swell of a worship song. Even with all this variety, we find that personal taste is the final arbiter in our choice of hymns. Sentiments that make some uncomfortable may be perfectly acceptable to others. Does this mean that we should count only hymns that we "like" as relevant? This seems to me a dangerous path to follow. Hymns at their best are works of performance art and can, like plays, be reinvigorated by the style of performance. They can be stored away, yet taken out on any given occasion. However, they form part of a living tradition which continues to flourish even in these times of dwindling church numbers. As hymn singers with a vast store of texts in our hearts and minds, we have a responsibility to maintain this tradition and ensure that it is safeguarded for future generations. In this store are our Christmas hymns. Sadly, regarded by some as tainted with over-familiarity, these are often branded as "the usual suspects". For me, the main difficulty with this point of view is that it does not allow those coming to a hymn for the first time to make up their own minds. Furthermore, for some singers, far from being the "usual suspects", these hymns are old friends that they meet up with each year and perhaps even discover a side to them that they had never seen before.

An example of such a "usual suspect" is "Once in royal David's city" (Mrs C. F. Alexander), a Christmas favourite that opens the *Nine Lessons and Carols* service broadcast every Christmas Eve from King's College, Cambridge. This tradition is a source of discomfort for some. First, on the ground of gender inequality: at the time of writing the choir of King's College does not admit girls or women. Second, the tradition of a robed choir is anathema to some. Third, the text, a Victorian hymn, comes under fire especially for the lines "Christian children, all must be mild, obedient, good as he". Why, the critics ask, should children be silent, and was not the infant Jesus as noisy as any other earthly baby? Is this hymn really a warning to children to be seen and not heard? I propose a different response. Perhaps Mrs Alexander was recognizing the simple fact that we are all children of God and, as such, are supposed to emulate Jesus by being "good". In many hymnbooks, this offending line has been reworked, or omitted, and it is impossible to judge which one is the "right" version for singers today. However, as the solo treble leads the journey down the nave of King's College Chapel, our conscientious qualms about sentiment or language seem to dissolve in the moment.

Critics of Christmas hymns such as "Once in royal David's city" denounce them as self-indulgent and would prefer to silence what they see as sentimental twaddle. It would certainly be easy simply to stop singing hymns that we find old-fashioned in favour of something completely new, or perhaps even nothing at all. However, if we are tempted to replace these well-loved vintage hymns, along with their deep-rooted associations, we may lose more than we bargained for. Archaic though these traditions may look to some modern eyes, they still occupy a significant place in our culture and can be anchored there only through repetition and familiarity. We in Britain are lucky to have free speech and to be able to express ourselves within the bounds of good taste and respect for others. Elsewhere people are not always so fortunate, and I have seen at first-hand what happens if hymn singing—or indeed any cultural activity—is stifled. I visited Timisoara, Romania, in 2005 to take part in a hymn conference. Still in the shadow of Ceausescu's punitive regime, which had ended with the revolution in 1989, people remained wary of admitting to the importance of Christian hymns in their lives. One of the conference papers in particular drew attention to the dire plight of Christmas carols in Romania. It transpired that an ethnomusicologist was working against the clock and travelling round the country collecting carols—both the words and the music—before they vanished from the country's heritage. The urgency arose from the fact that no new singers had learned carols during the forty-two years of Communist rule in Romania because children were not taught their traditional hymns. The carols themselves remained only as a quickly disappearing oral tradition. While it is unlikely that this disaster will befall our hymns in Britain, it is only by giving children the opportunity to learn our vintage hymns that they will be preserved for posterity as a living tradition. The lone treble in King's College each year carries the torch for us all. In tossing aside a vintage hymn in favour of something new we are in danger of cutting ourselves off from yet another rich stream in our history.

Conclusion

This exploration of our hymn-singing tradition has revealed how complex it is to decide whether a vintage hymn is relevant or not. However, one simple truth has emerged from our discussion—that when we sing hymns together, enjoying these words and wedded to this music, we are drawn together, shoulder to shoulder, in solidarity. How sad, then, to see how the COVID-19 pandemic has robbed us of this collective activity and swept away centuries of tradition in a few short months! Now deemed too dangerous for worshippers to meet, entry to churches has been restricted and services have been largely relegated to the internet. Even singing in schools and choirs has been suppressed. Sadly, hymn singing is not the only shared activity that has been curtailed, and to many it seems that all these social pleasures we used to enjoy have been stolen from us. We have yet to count the cost of what our communities have lost!

It is no trivial matter that we need to work to keep our vintage hymns alive in our hearts and minds. Perhaps it is overstating the case to say that if these hymns are not sung regularly, they will disappear from the repertoire with the possible result that all record of them will be lost. We have already established that they are safeguarded in our hymnbooks. Hymns, though, are not fossils to be admired in a display case. They are alive—but only if they are sung. We observed that we learned many of the hymns we know and love when we were children, yet if children no longer hear and sing them, the dust will surely gather on the collection.

There is much that we have lost through the pandemic, including thousands of lives, and some may think that to lose a few hymns is a minor matter. However, we are, in the main, social beings; a vital part of our cultural identity is maintained by the activities we pursue together—playing sport, dancing, attending football matches, watching plays and films together and—yes— singing hymns. Any long-term threat to these activities may serve to undermine our cultural identity. It has become apparent that vintage hymns may have features which we value and also features that give us pause. Nevertheless, we have seen that hymns that trouble us can, in their very shortcomings, throw a spotlight on attitudes and prejudices that were once widely shared and created few qualms in singers at the time they were written. Not only do these hymns shine a light on our past attitudes, but they can also serve as a warning not to let ourselves acquire new prejudices as pernicious as those that we now reject. The vintage hymns that express sentiments which we endorse wholeheartedly are important not only because they enshrine moral or religious truths, but because they also allow us to give voice to these beliefs in the company of others.

Perhaps our hymn-singing tradition can be likened to a many-stranded cord that links us to the past. No single strand stretches from one end to the other but, woven together, each secures the whole. Carelessly snap this strand or that and we jeopardize the safety of all. Likewise, our hymns—whether those we most treasure or those we least admire—are the strands in this cord that binds us to the past in a living tradition made up of old hymns and new. Who would want to lose this vital link with our past? As Bunty Newport writes:

Think of a world without any poetry
Think of a book without any words
Think of a song without any music
Think of a hymn without any verse.

All things bright and beautiful—a case study

The search to discover whether this hymn or that is relevant to singers today began with "All things bright and beautiful". We have seen that this search is not easy. There are many things to take into account when judging a hymn: some things weigh in its favour whereas others will weigh against it. Which way will the scales fall? "All things bright and beautiful" is a striking example of this—a hymn which is both loved and hated in equal measure. I feel, though, that this hymn has much to offer us today and remains a highly relevant text. We know that a hymn can be viewed from both the historical point at which it was written and from the point of view of later singers who sing with the priorities of their own age. It is well-known that Mrs Alexander wrote the hymn for children to illustrate aspects of Christian belief. It was first published in *Hymns for Little Children* (1848) and has remained in print ever since. From a historical point of view, there are undoubtedly some dated modes of expression and imagery, but for singers today, far from being old-fashioned, "All things bright and beautiful" has pride of place amongst our vintage hymns and continues to be effective. It serves both its original purpose of teaching children and, for modern singers, I shall argue, it invites us to face up to some of the gravest issues in the world today.

In our challenging times, there is doom and gloom all around and despondency clouds the future. There are dire warnings concerning our rapidly declining resources along with fears over food poverty, climate change and diminishing biodiversity. On the other hand, "life-style" and spiritual gurus are continually exhorting us to focus on ourselves and cultivate our own well-being. Books tell us how we can organize our cupboards, improve relationships, maintain that all-important work-life balance and enjoy wild adventure holidays. How can we handle this cacophony of competing messages? One response is to pay attention to the world around us, which is exactly what Mrs Alexander encourages us to do. As I lead you on a journey through the hymn, unpacking some of the ideas and images along the way, we shall discover not only how Mrs Alexander reminds us of the miracle of creation but also, as if writing today, she sounds a warning with her recognition of the fragility of the natural world. In singing "All things bright and beautiful" today, we are urged to shoulder our responsibilities as caretakers of our beautiful planet. By the end of this case study, I hope you will see this much-maligned hymn in an altogether new light.

It seems prudent to deal first with the verse that is the most frequent target of enemy fire:

> The rich man in his castle,
> the poor man at his gate;
> God made them, high or lowly,
> and ordered their estate.

Mrs Alexander, even though she gave to various philanthropic causes, lived in a time of rigid social hierarchy with the fortunate at the top of the pile and the less fortunate at the bottom. It is therefore no surprise that she expresses herself in those terms. She was a staunch supporter of the establishment and benefited as a member of the dominant Protestant elite, while the poor were left to suffer as a result of the potato famine. It would seem that, even though this verse has not been included in printed hymnbooks for many years, there lingers an intense dislike of it. The verse's omission was mentioned as long ago as 1961 by Barbara Pym in her novel *No Fond Return of Love*. The main character, Dulcie, stands to sing in a "loud indignant voice, waiting for the lines . . . but they never came . . . She sat down, feeling cheated of her indignation".[12]

Many people share Dulcie's opposition to the verse. Whilst rejoicing that it is no longer included in hymnbooks, there remains a strong desire to speak up against inequality—and what better way than to pick an argument with a verse from a hymn? There have been, however, in recent years, some spirited defences of the verse. Timothy Dudley-Smith, for example, in his *A Functional Art: Reflections of a Hymn Writer*, whilst not defending the verse, is inclined to shift the blame for its hostile reception on to careless hymnbook editors. He points out that it is easy to misinterpret the text. He writes:

> . . . the hymn is about creation, God as maker: indeed, the word, "made" comes in every sentence. The second clue lies in the comma in the middle of line three. It throws the emphasis onto the words "God made them", so that whether we are rich or poor, all are equal in God's creation; and this is simply borrowing from Scripture: "The rich and poor meet together; the Lord is the maker of them all."[13]

Dudley-Smith suggests that, seen in this light, the hymn levels rather than divides the population. However, it may occur to one that he fails to comment on the word "ordered" with its implication that it is by divine diktat that some are welcomed to a wealthy elite whilst others are destined to suffer without complaint.

This verse invites us to explore how difficult it is to establish the relevance of a hymn. Although an "All things bright and beautiful" which includes this verse receives a poor press, there can be no question that it is known and loved by many. For this reason alone, it is likely that it will continue to be sung. The common solution is to sing the hymn minus the offending verse. This means that we preserve a vintage hymn which continues to fulfil its original purpose. An alternative suggestion is to keep this difficult verse whilst acknowledging, along with Dulcie, its frankly uncomfortable sentiments. Of course, it is unlikely that anyone will want to keep the verse, but it is worth considering. Revisiting painful aspects of our past can serve as a stark warning should history fail to learn its lesson. Yet another response could be to reverse the sense of this troubling verse. Michael Forster (b. 1946) has done just this in his hymn "The rich in splendid castle homes":

> The rich in splendid castle homes
> The poor ones at the gate,
> God has created equally,
> and hates their current state.[14]

Singing such a hymn presents the opportunity to consider the highly relevant topics of social justice and equality.

In spite of the discomfort over this verse, "All things bright and beautiful" resonates across the generations. It is sung on numerous occasions in both secular and sacred venues and is published in countless hymnbooks as well as springing up in popular culture. Only recently I was reading a tense detective novel called *The Crossing Places* by Elly Griffiths (2010). In one episode "All things bright and beautiful" is mentioned alongside other popular hymns including Sydney Carter's "Lord of the dance". Griffiths is a well-known crime writer, and her novels are full of contemporary detail. She was confident, clearly, that even her non-churchgoing readers were sure to know the hymns.

Even so, choosing "All things bright and beautiful" for a baptism, wedding or funeral is frequently met with a snort of derision. One reason for this could be simply that adult singers see it as just another old-fashioned children's hymn decked out with bland images of nature—a hymn that certainly has nothing to teach us today. However, as I said before, looked at with modern eyes, it is possible to interpret it as a warning to value the fragile wonders of our beautiful world and take care of its dwindling resources. How interesting it is to see in recent protests over climate change it is youth that is taking the lead. It is the fresh eyes of young people, not the blinkered eyes of jaded politicians, that have seen most clearly what must be done to preserve our environment. At times, we must acknowledge, as Wordsworth wrote, that "The child is father to the man".

Before we start looking at the text in detail, let's make some "broad brush" observations. On one level, a text of thankfulness, "All things bright and beautiful" forms a bridge from the microscopic to the cosmic. It is a hymn that begs singers to look up, look down and look around, or as C. S. Lewis writes: "The only imperative that nature utters is, 'Look. Listen. Attend.'".[15] This movement of thought is found in many other hymns. For example, "Glad that I live am I" pictures how faith grows as the worshipper looks from the tiny drops of dew to the wide-open skies. Again, a more recent hymn, "I nearly forgot to say thank you" (John Gowans, 1934–2012), also moves from the big to the small, from the rare to the ordinary.

Looking afresh at "All things bright and beautiful", it can be seen to resonate with singers today. The first verse relies heavily on the idea of smallness:

> Each little flower that opens
> each little bird that sings
> he made their glowing colours
> he made their tiny wings.

Critics of the hymn have made this verse the object of their scorn, and there are many articles referring to the saccharine and twee nature of the lines, although less hostile commentators suggest that Mrs Alexander is simply making the outside world accessible to children and points out they enjoy the littleness of "little" things. There is some truth in this, as anyone on a country walk with a toddler will attest when presented with a single daisy or leaf. But there is even more to be found in this verse. All the observations of nature are preceded by the word "each", which suggests "each and every" and invites us to appreciate the myriad of small things, so easily overlooked, that surround us. Small in size certainly does not mean small in significance. As William Blake wrote:

> To see a World in a Grain of Sand
> and Heaven in a Wild Flower
> Hold Infinity in the palm of your hand
> and Eternity in an hour.[16]

And what of those "glowing colours"? We have noted already how important is the vocabulary of nature, and colour is a vital element in this. According to Robert Macfarlane, for example, children are more likely to be able to identify the names of Pokémon characters than the common features of the field and woods. Put quite simply, if our attention is no longer drawn to "glowing colours" we have less reason to look up and see the beauty around us.

Continuing with the theme of smallness, Mrs Alexander does not neglect the "tiny wings" which come in each refrain. Once more the word "tiny" comes in for a pasting from the hymn police—it is twee, they claim, and celebrates the trivial. Tiny wings can certainly be a nuisance if, belonging to insects, they interfere with our perfectly shaped vegetables and beautifully manicured lawns! Now, though, we are starting to realize that they are vital for biodiversity as well as for pollination. Insects are little regarded since it is much more appealing to direct our efforts into preserving cuddly mammals or the big game of the deserts and savannas. Oh dear! Studies of recent years have drawn attention to the fact that the world's insects are hurtling down the path to extinction, threatening a catastrophic collapse of nature's ecosystems. Analysis has found that many species are in decline and could vanish completely within a century. Therefore, Mrs Alexander's reference to "tiny wings", far from celebrating the trivial, reminds us that insects are vital to our food chain. Their loss would, of course, mean irreparable harm to the diets of all other living things. If we do not keep these "tiny wings" in the forefront of our minds, for example when we sing our hymns, is there not a danger that they might cease to exist, taking humanity with them? Once more: "Think of a world without any flowers"!

Having considered the smallest creatures in the first verse of "All things bright and beautiful", Mrs Alexander turns her attention to nature on a grander scale in the second verse:

> The purple-headed mountain,
> the river running by,
> the sunset, and the morning
> that brightens up the sky.

Whilst it is entirely possible that Mrs Alexander was thinking of a mountain close to home, for singers today, mountains have come to mean the allure of remote places. Recent trends encouraging extreme travel afford plenty of opportunity for exploring mountains. Indeed the "bucket list" books, websites and podcasts include adventure and climbing on their "must do" lists. Perhaps the desire for distant places is inborn? As Cecily Taylor

(1930–2018) writes in her challenging reworking of the words of Chief Seattle: "We belong to the mountains and the plains".

For Mrs Alexander, the mountains are, perhaps, both in the distance and close to home. Some contemporary collections, notably *Singing the Faith*, have tinkered with the text so that the "purple-headed mountain" is merely "purple-heathered". While this draws on a familiar image, it detracts from the original by encouraging us to look down at our feet rather than up to the vistas beyond.

The mountain does seem to offer the promise of an exotic adventure, but the third verse of the hymn has particular urgency for singers today. The first two lines could serve to remind us of the pressing debate on climate change:

> The cold wind in the winter,
> the pleasant summer sun . . .

What is the weather for us today? As adults we have become familiar with following the progress of weather through regular bulletins on computer and television. Storms are even given names—a trend which, according to some studies, is supposed to make us take their threat more seriously. Are storms becoming our friends—or our enemies? Have they become acquaintances whom we can introduce cosily into conversations as if they were simply dropping round for a cup of tea? Or are they adversaries with whom we must enter into combat? Children, though, are encouraged to enjoy the weather and to sing about it in playful terms. Think, for example, of Gwendoline Smith's (1909–95) ditty:

> I love the sun it shines on me,
> God made the sun and God made me.

More eloquent is Shelley's "Spirit of delight":

> I love snow, and all the forms
> of radiant frost;
> I love waves, and winds and storms,
> everything almost
> which is nature's and maybe
> untainted by man's misery.

Extreme weather has suddenly made us realize what the effects of climate change will be. This looming crisis has been much in the news in more recent times following unprecedented protest marches which have brought city centres to a standstill. This grass-roots movement was inspired by Greta Thunberg, a sixteen-year-old Swedish activist who began her campaign by staging lone sit-ins every Friday afternoon. The burden of the urgent message comes from school-age students demanding that adult politicians start taking responsibility for the havoc caused to our climate by the thoughtlessness of an unreflecting adult population which the children of today will be forced to endure when they are adults themselves. Again Cecily Taylor speaks through Chief Seattle:

> Listen to our children and their children
> pleading for life's legacy so that we have to give.
> Listen now and hurry—use the fleeting minutes;
> if we heed the Wise One now, humanity could live.

If the planet is disrupted by global warming, what will happen to our food resources? Once again we can read a warning for our times—though, of course, this was unforeseen by Mrs Alexander at the time of writing—as we move to the second half of this verse:

> The ripe fruits in the garden
> he made them every one.

Although, as we have seen, there is a lively interest in people "growing their own", the wider picture is far bleaker. What about the parlous state of food production in the twenty-first century? It is becoming clear that the world's capacity to produce food is being undermined by humanity's failure to protect biodiversity. This is happening because farms, cities and factories gobble up land and pump out chemicals. Forests, grassland, coral reefs and seagrass beds are being depleted, while a third of our seas are being over-fished. Mrs Alexander's hymn can serve to heighten our awareness of the threat to bounteous nature. The debate is crucial, and as we sing this single line of "All things bright and beautiful", we can go some way towards keeping such vital matters at the forefront of our minds.

Of all the verses in "All things bright and beautiful" it is perhaps the fourth verse that has been subjected to the harshest criticism:

> The tall trees in the greenwood,
> the meadows for our play,
> the rushes by the water
> to gather every day.

Perhaps hostility to this verse is prompted by a suspicion that it conjures up the vision of an impossible pastoral idyll—a golden past that may have never existed and is, at any rate, quite out of keeping with our busy modern lives. We don't have time to "play" in the meadows—or anywhere else for that matter! Play is all very well for children who have nothing better to do until they are old enough to suffer a rigorous testing regime: a painful and stressful round of exams all aimed at university entrance and job security. Perhaps Mrs Alexander realized, however, that "play" is not just a frivolous interruption to our day-to-day lives, but a crucial part of growing as human beings. There are ample studies to suggest that playing is a necessary part of growing up, yet it is an activity squeezed out on the one hand by imagined dangers and on the other hand by the demands of an ever-expanding curriculum. Indeed, a recent study has drawn attention to the fact that children are experiencing shrinking breaktimes in their school day. In these pressured times, leisure has been reduced to goal-based activities including "apps" that track actions on our mobile phones, giving us "likes" and "kudos". As W. H. Davies wrote, it is:

> A poor life, this, if, full of care
> we have no time to stand and stare . . .

There is constant talk about gaining resilience—yet instances of anxiety disorders and depression are rising in all sections of society. Perhaps it is time to take the risk of climbing those tall trees? What could be better than an impromptu game of football in the meadow with jumpers for goal posts and—as Estelle White writes in her wonderfully evocative text "Autumn days when the grass is jewelled"—"a win for my home team".

Having examined "All things bright and beautiful" in some detail, it seems clear to me that it is a relevant text if ever there was one! The fact that it appears in at least ninety-seven hymnbooks all published in the twentieth and twenty-first centuries is unequivocal evidence of its enduring popularity. Despite the mockery heaped upon it, "All things bright and beautiful" survives.

Sung with fresh voices, then, "All things bright and beautiful" shows us a beautiful world—but a world in crisis. Here we have a hymn which was gifted to us by a writer who, even in her enthusiasm for educating children in the tenets of the Christian faith, could have little imagined what it would mean to future singers over 150 years later. By appreciating this hymn in its nineteenth-century context, together with its contemporary resonance, we have every reason to keep singing it. Yes, it may be associated with a long-gone social hierarchy; yes, it may be over-sung and over-familiar; yet for all that, "All things bright and beautiful" has the power to inspire new thinking. Let's preserve this vintage hymn by singing it with gusto.

How times have changed since I first conceived the idea of this book! Sadly, singing anything "with gusto" is now, as a result of the COVID-19 pandemic, no longer possible in any social situation. Instead we are forced to acknowledge that the hymn singing we enjoy—at school, in church and on our special family occasions—is a thing of the past. Looking to the future, we ask ourselves whether communal hymn singing will ever be part of our lives again. In fact, coronavirus has substantially altered our attitude to meeting socially at all. Eating together, watching films together and singing together are all now rare and dangerous activities! On a practical level the necessary screens, masks and distance requirements have robbed so many activities of any spontaneity and many centuries of lifting our voices together is already a distant memory. What can we do to ensure that hymn singing does not fade to a fond memory but remains a living tradition? Where can we find a haven in these uncharted waters? For hymn singers a still centre can be found in the rich hoard of vintage texts ever ready to find their voice.

Hymnbooks mentioned

Sunday School Praise (London: National Sunday School Union, 1958).

Pilgrim Praise (London: Galliard, 1972).

With One Voice (London: Harper Collins, 1979).

Hymns & Psalms: A Methodist and Ecumenical Hymnbook (Peterborough: Methodist Publishing House, 1983).

Baptist Praise and Worship (Oxford: Oxford University Press, 1991).

Carols Old and New (Stowmarket: Kevin Mayhew, 1991).

Complete Anglican Hymns Old & New (Stowmarket: Kevin Mayhew, 2000).

Mission Praise 30th Anniversary Version (London: Harper Collins, 2004).

Hymns We Have Always Loved (Stowmarket: Kevin Mayhew, 2005).

Redemption Songs (London: Harper Collins, 2005).

Singing the Faith (Norwich: Canterbury Press, 2011).

Notes

1   Thomas Aquinas, *Exposition of the Psalms of David*, Introduction.

2   Samuel Butler, *The Way of All Flesh* (London: Washington Square, 1873), p. 58.

3   Mary Sheepshank, *A Price for Everything* (London: Black Swan, 1995), p. 163.

4   C. S. Lewis, *The Four Loves* (London: Geoffrey Bles, 1960), p. 8.

5   R. Macfarlene & J. Morris, *The Lost Words* (London: Hamish Hamilton, 2018), p. 1.

6   © 1973 A&C Black Ltd. Used with permission.

7   Percy Dearmer, *Songs of Praise Discussed* (Oxford: Oxford University Press, 1933), p. 271.

8   J. G. Farrell, *The Siege of Krishnapur* (London: Weidenfeld & Nicolson, 1973), p. 56.

9   Paul Scott, *The Towers of Silence* (London: Random House, 2005), p. 301.

10 Brian Wren, *What Language Shall I Borrow? God-talk in Worship: A Male Response to Feminist Theology* (London: SCM Press, 1989), p. 11.

11 Reproduced by kind permission of Sue Gilmurray.

12 Barbara Pym, *No Fond Return of Love* (London: Jonathan Cape, 1961), p. 27.

13 Timothy Dudley-Smith, *A Functional Art: Reflections of a Hymn Writer* (Oxford: Oxford University Press, 2017), p. 15.

14 © 1993 Kevin Mayhew Ltd.

15 Lewis, *The Four Loves*, p. 24.

16 William Blake, "Auguries of Innocence".

Lightning Source UK Ltd.
Milton Keynes UK
UKHW021246030621
384866UK00008B/66